▶ Zombie Talk

Other Palgrave Pivot titles

G. Douglas Atkins: **Strategy and Purpose in T.S. Eliot's Major Poems: Language, Hermeneutics, and Ancient Truth in "New Verse"**

Christophe Assens and Aline Courie Lemeur: **Networks Governance, Partnership Management and Coalitions Federation**

Katia Pilati: **Migrants' Political Participation in Exclusionary Contexts: From Subcultures to Radicalization**

Yvette Taylor: **Making Space for Queer-Identifying Religious Youth**

Andrew Smith: **Racism and Everyday Life: Social Theory, History and 'Race'**

Othon Anastasakis, David Madden, and Elizabeth Roberts: **Balkan Legacies of the Great War: The Past is Never Dead**

Garold Murray and Naomi Fujishima: **Social Spaces for Language Learning: Stories from the L-café**

Sarah Kember: **iMedia: The Gendering of Objects, Environments and Smart Materials**

Kevin Blackburn: **War, Sport and the Anzac Tradition**

Jackie Dickenson: **Australian Women in Advertising in the Twentieth Century**

Russell Blackford: **The Mystery of Moral Authority**

Harold D. Clarke, Peter Kellner, Marianne Stewart, Joe Twyman and Paul Whiteley: **Austerity and Political Choice in Britain**

Jonas Campion and Xavier Rousseaux (editors): **Policing New Risks in Modern European History**

Amelia Manuti and Pasquale Davide de Palma: **The Social Organization: Managing Human Capital through Social Media**

Piyush Tiwari (editor): **The Towers of New Capital: Mega Townships in India**

Indranarain Ramlall: **Central Bank Ratings: A New Methodology for Global Excellence**

Stephen Paul Miller: **The New Deal as a Triumph of Social Work: Frances Perkins and the Confluence of Early Twentieth Century Social Work with Mid-Twentieth Century Politics and Government**

Nicholas Pamment: **Community Reparation for Young Offenders: Perceptions, Policy and Practice**

David F. Tennant and Marlon R. Tracey: **Sovereign Debt and Credit Rating Bias**

Jefferson Walker: **King Returns to Washington: Explorations of Memory, Rhetoric, and Politics in the Martin Luther King, Jr.** National Memorial

palgrave▶pivot

Zombie Talk: Culture, History, Politics

David R. Castillo
*Professor of Romance Languages and Literatures,
State University of New York at Buffalo, USA*

David Schmid
*Associate Professor of English,
State University of New York at Buffalo, USA*

David A. Reilly
*Professor and Chair, Department of Political Science,
Niagara University, USA*

and

John Edgar Browning
*Marion L. Brittain Postdoctoral Fellow,
Georgia Institute of Technology, USA*

ZOMBIE TALK
Copyright © David R. Castillo, David Schmid, David A. Reilly and John Edgar Browning, 2016.
Afterword © William Egginton, 2016.

All rights reserved. No reproduction, copy or transmission of this publication may be made without written permission.

No portion of this publication may be reproduced, copied or transmitted save with written permission. In accordance with the provisions of the Copyright, Designs and Patents Act 1988, or under the terms of any licence permitting limited copying issued by the Copyright Licensing Agency, Saffron House, 6–10 Kirby Street, London EC1N 8TS.

Any person who does any unauthorized act in relation to this publication may be liable to criminal prosecution and civil claims for damages.

First published 2016 by
PALGRAVE MACMILLAN

The authors have asserted their rights to be identified as the authors of this work in accordance with the Copyright, Designs and Patents Act 1988.

Palgrave Macmillan in the UK is an imprint of Macmillan Publishers Limited, registered in England, company number 785998, of Houndmills, Basingstoke, Hampshire RG21 6XS.

Palgrave Macmillan in the US is a division of Nature America, Inc., One New York Plaza, Suite 4500 New York, NY 10004-1562.

Palgrave Macmillan is the global academic imprint of the above companies and has companies and representatives throughout the world.

Hardback ISBN: 978-1-137-57524-1
E-PUB ISBN: 978-1-137-56774-1
E-PDF ISBN: 978-1-137-56772-7
DOI: 10.1057/9781137567727

Distribution in the UK, Europe and the rest of the world is by Palgrave Macmillan®, a division of Macmillan Publishers Limited, registered in England, company number 785998, of Houndmills, Basingstoke, Hampshire RG21 6XS.

Library of Congress Cataloging-in-Publication Data is available from the Library of Congress

A catalog record for this book is available from the Library of Congress

A catalogue record for the book is available from the British Library

For
Wes Craven (1939–2015),
whose favorite horror film was Night of the Living Dead

Contents

Acknowledgments	vii
Notes on the Authors	viii
Introduction: Our Zombies, Our Remnants *David R. Castillo and John Edgar Browning*	1
1 Survival Horrors, Survival Spaces: Tracing the Modern Zombie (Cine)Myth through to the Postmillennium *John Edgar Browning*	9
2 Zombie Masses: Monsters for the Age of Global Capitalism *David R. Castillo*	39
3 The Coming Apocalypses of Zombies and Globalization *David A. Reilly*	63
4 The Limits of Zombies: Monsters for a Neoliberal Age *David Schmid*	92
Afterword: What Are We Talking About When We Talk About Zombies? *William Egginton*	108
Bibliography	115
Index	127

Acknowledgments

This research was sponsored by the Cultures and Texts Strategic Strength and the Office of the Associate Vice President for Research Advancement and Strategic Initiatives, University at Buffalo, The State University of New York, USA.

Chapter 1. "Survival Horrors, Survival Spaces: Tracing the Modern Zombie (Cine)Myth through to the Postmillennium" is an expanded version of "Survival Horrors, Survival Spaces: Tracing the Modern Zombie (Cine)Myth," which originally appeared in *Horror Studies* 2, no. 1 (May 2011): 41–59.

Chapter 2. "Zombie Masses: Monsters for the Age of Global Capitalism" is an expanded version of the online paper "Monsters for the Age of the Post-human," which originally appeared in *Writing Monsters: Essays on Iberian and Latin American Cultures*, eds. Adriana Gordillo and Nicholas Spadaccini, a themed issue of *Hispanic Issues On Line* 15 (Spring 2014): 161–78.

Notes on the Authors

John Edgar Browning (Ph.D., SUNY-Buffalo, USA) is a Marion L. Brittain Postdoctoral Fellow in the School of Literature, Media, and Communication at the Georgia Institute of Technology, USA. He has contracted or co-/written more than 12 books, including (with Caroline J. S. Picart) *Speaking of Monsters: A Teratological Anthology* (Palgrave Macmillan, 2012) and *The Forgotten Writings of Bram Stoker* (Palgrave Macmillan, 2012), and contracted or published more than 50 articles, book chapters, and reviews on subjects that cluster around cultural theory, horror, vampires, Bram Stoker, and the Gothic. He has also appeared as a guest academic scholar on National Geographic's *Taboo USA* (2013–) and The Discovery Channel's *William Shatner's Weird or What?* (2010–) to discuss vampires. Presently, he is an associate editor for the open access journal *Palgrave Communications* and serves on the editorial and advisory boards of *The Journal of Positive Sexuality* and the Series in *Law, Culture and the Humanities*, Fairleigh Dickinson University Press.

David R. Castillo (Ph.D., University of Minnesota, USA) is Professor and former Chair of the Romance Languages and Literatures Department at SUNY-Buffalo, USA. He is the author of *(A)Wry Views: Anamorphosis, Cervantes, and the Early Picaresque* (Purdue University Press, 2001) and *Baroque Horrors: Roots of the Fantastic in the Age of Curiosities* (2010, reprinted in paperback in 2012). Castillo is also co-editor of *Reason and Its Others: Italy, Spain, and the New World* (2006) and *Spectacle and Topophilia: Reading Early and*

Postmodern Hispanic Cultures (2012). In addition, Castillo has published some 40 essays on different aspects of early modern literature and baroque and neo-baroque culture. His current research includes a new book project (co-authored with William Egginton) entitled *Medialogies: Reading Reality in the Age of Inflationary Media* (forthcoming 2017) and a co-edited volume tentatively titled *Writing in the End of Times*.

William Egginton (Ph.D., Stanford University, USA) is Andrew W. Mellon Professor of Humanities and Professor of German and Romance Languages and Literatures at Johns Hopkins University, USA. He is the author of numerous books, papers, articles, blogs, and translations, including *How the World Became a Stage* (2003), *Perversity and Ethics* (2005), *A Wrinkle in History (Contemporary European Cultural Studies)* (2007), *The Philosopher's Desire: Psychoanalysis, Interpretation, and Truth* (2007), *The Theater of Truth: The Ideology of (Neo)Baroque Aesthetics* (2009), and *In Defense of Religious Moderation* (2011). He is also co-editor (with David E. Johnson) of *Thinking with Borges* (2009) and (with Mike Sandbothe) *The Pragmatic Turn in Philosophy: Contemporary Engagements Between Analytic and Continental Thought* (2004), and translator of Lisa Block de Behar's *Borges: The Passion of an Endless Quotation (SUNY Series in Latin American and Iberian Thought and Culture)* (2002, 2nd edition 2013). His most recent book is *The Man Who Invented Fiction: How Cervantes Ushered in the Modern World* (2016).

David A. Reilly (Ph.D., University of Colorado, USA) is Professor and Chair in the Department of Political Science, and Director of International Studies at Niagara University, USA. The major focus of his research has been how ideas and information (and now zombies) flow across borders. He examines how states' decisions are affected by their environment and their neighbors. In this context, his research has addressed democratization, human rights, cooperation, and conflict. Reilly's publications include works in *World Politics*, *Geopolitics*, *Conflict Resolution Quarterly*, *International Studies Review*, *Journal of Conflict Studies*, and *East European Politics and Societies*. He has also published on pedagogy in *PS: Political Science & Politics*, *Simulation and Gaming*, and recently served as the president of the Active Learning in International Affairs section of the International Studies Association.

David Schmid (Ph.D., Stanford University, USA), born and raised in England, is Associate Professor in the Department of English at

SUNY-Buffalo, USA. The winner of the Milton Plesur and the SUNY Chancellor's Awards for Excellence in Teaching, Schmid teaches courses in British and American fiction, cultural studies, and popular culture. He is the author of *Natural Born Celebrities: Serial Killers in American Culture* (2005), and he has published on a variety of subjects, including the nonfiction novel, celebrity, film adaptation, *Dracula*, and crime fiction, in such journals as *Literature/Film Quarterly*, *The Australasian Journal of Popular Culture*, and *The Journal of American Culture*. He is also editor of the two-volume anthology *Violence in American Popular Culture* (2015) and co-editor (with Andrew Pepper) of *Globalization and the State in Contemporary Crime Fiction* (Palgrave Macmillan, forthcoming). He is currently completing a single-authored monograph entitled *From the Locked Room to the Globe: Space in Crime Fiction*.

Introduction: Our Zombies, Our Remnants

David R. Castillo and John Edgar Browning

Abstract: *Beginning with the claim that the interdisciplinary discussions herein are grounded on three basic observations, this collaborative volume has been, at its core, driven by a sense of timeliness and urgency tied to the shared conviction that* media literacy *is of the utmost importance today, as our lives are increasingly framed by all manner of screens and indeed ruled by optical codes generated and reified by these screens. The incredible advances seen in Zombie Studies in the last decade are still being measured, and as this introduction outlines, chapter by chapter, we here take advantage of this moment by examining the zombie phenomenon in context while incorporating, simultaneously, a good number of recent studies and popular works of literary and cinematic fiction.*

Castillo, David R., David Schmid, David A. Reilly and John Edgar Browning. *Zombie Talk: Culture, History, Politics.* New York: Palgrave Macmillan, 2016.
DOI: 10.1057/9781137567727.0004.

The interdisciplinary discussions included in this volume are grounded on three basic observations: (1) The pervasive presence of the zombie *topos* in the present multi-media culture is virtually unprecedented; (2) scholarly attempts to foster and encourage media literacy today must therefore engage this omnipresent *topos*; and (3) in its modern format the zombie *topos* comes with (post)apocalyptic landscapes and a sustained focus on the group dynamics of the survivors. At its core, this collaborative project has been driven, right from the start, by a sense of timeliness and urgency tied to the shared conviction that *media literacy* is of the utmost importance today, as our lives are increasingly framed by all manner of screens and indeed ruled by optical codes generated and reified by these screens.

We are hardly alone in recognizing the need for media literacy. In fact, the urgency of media literacy training is beginning to be acknowledged outside of the humanistic fields of literature, media, and culture studies; in social science disciplines; and even among legal scholars. Thus, NYU Law professor Richard K. Sherwin, for example, has devoted an entire monographic study to illustrate the pressing need for "visual literacy training" for legal professionals, as well as for the public at large, as our legal system, our individual and collective sense of justice, and even the scope of our imagination are increasingly influenced by and literally framed by screens. As he writes:

> How and what people see (and fail to see) varies from place to place and time to time. Social conventions frame the visible and invisible alike—establishing the one by virtue of the other.... How visual meaning making occurs, how (and with what aesthetic and ethic consequences) it constructs a world, a self, and a network of relations for us to be in, is not obvious. Critical self-reflexiveness and prudence in judgment presuppose visual literacy, and visual literacy, like its literary counterpart, does not simply happen. It requires conscientious training.[1]

In his concluding remarks this law scholar asks a key question: "Who and what do we become when we live on the screen, when we internalize the screen's optical code as our own?"[2]

Remarkably, George A. Romero's landmark films seem to offer a series of nightmarish responses to this question. If in *Dawn of the Dead* (1978), Romero planted the suggestion that *the zombies are us*, insatiable masses of mindless, soulless, destructive consumers, in *Land of the Dead* (2005), he explicitly links the absolute lack of awareness of the zombie masses to the hypnotic and disarming power of the light shows to which they are subjected, the "sky flowers" deployed by mercenaries of the shopping mall to keep them distracted, unware of their surroundings, even of their own destruction.

With these films in mind and other self-reflective products of the zombie genre, the authors of the present volume explore the uneasy and in some ways contradictory relation that the current zombie culture maintains with the global mass-media industry. The idea that the mass-media industry is at the root of modern and now post-modern processes of *dehumanization* can be traced back to the Marxist critique of capitalist modernity, most notoriously to the philosophers and critics associated with the Frankfurt school, Theodor Adorno and Max Horkheimer among them. Yet, what is peculiar and specific about recent iterations of these notions in mainstream cultural commentary, as well as in more specialized circles of ideological criticism, is what we might call "the apocalyptic turn" of the discussion. If New York Times best-selling author Nicholas Carr wonders whether humanity can indeed survive the viral spreading of screens in his aptly titled book *The Glass Cage: Automation and Us* (2014), high theorists such as Slavoj Žižek note that it seems much easier today to picture the end of humanity, and indeed the end of all life on Earth, than a relatively modest change in the global economic structures that continue to damage the planet's environment (possibly beyond repair) while generating an endless stream of human and material debris.

The monstrous nature of global capitalism and its dominant neoliberal ideology and the framing function of its media industry receive sustained attention in our book, especially in chapters 2 and 4, which put the spotlight on familiar forms of economic and cultural traffic. To return to Romero's filmic vocabulary in *Land of the Dead*, the world is ruled by a monstrous master-class of CEOs and elite consumers who have barricaded themselves inside a high-end shopping mall surrounded by ruthless mercenaries who do their bidding. The third (outer) circle is populated by zombie masses. No wonder we root for the undead hordes led by a black zombie as they begin to acquire both a class consciousness and a sense of who the real enemy is and especially when they invade the exclusive (membership only) shopping mall and immolate the obscene bodies that inhabit it!

In a *New York Times* article entitled, "The Perils of Perfection," Evgeny Morozov warns the public against the Orwellian nightmare of panoptic digital technologies in the service of capitalist dreams of leveling perfection. Morozov discusses the futurist plans of digital technology moguls including the development of reality-altering devices such as smart glasses or contact lenses that would ideally serve to edit "disturbing sights" like "homeless people."[3] The point we make here is that in our mass-media culture the human and material debris generated by global economic structures is already virtually invisible. Could it be that the undead masses that come back to haunt us in zombie movies represent, in some way, this human and material debris that has been edited out of our field of vision? This would be consistent with the standard psychoanalytic explanation of horror fiction as the site of *the return of the repressed*.

Beyond the scope of the Romero classics and their racially and politically charged imagery, if there's something that most products of the current multimedia zombie culture have in common, it is the apocalyptic landscapes associated with the uprising of the dead. Indeed, as modern nightmares go, the zombie masses seem inextricably connected with end-of-times scenarios. No horsemen needed in this (post)modern version of the apocalypse; post-human walkers will do!

At the same time, the zombie-plagued landscape represents a kind of desperate hope for the rebirth of humanity out of the most radical state of nature that we can conceive. Accordingly, the zombie apocalypse is often reimagined as the necessary violent and unavoidably traumatic zero-point that severs us from the zombifying routines of our seemingly safe but automated and ultimately empty existence. This zero-point may be envisioned as an opportunity to rethink not just the *individual* but the *collective* as well, as the human survivors struggle to recreate a sense of community following the catastrophic collapse of all political and civic institutions. These notions are present throughout the book, most explicitly in chapters 1 and 3 which retrace the origins of the *survival space* in zombie fiction focusing not only on questions of literary and cinematic history but also on the political and ethical dilemmas that emerge within "survival spaces" in the post-Matheson and post-Romero zombie culture.

While these are some of the conceptual and thematic threads of the volume, the authors start with the most basic questions suggested by the unprecedented success of the zombie genre. If we believe that *we are our nightmares*, as much as we are our hopes, our dreams, aspirations, and desires, then it befits us to ask: What is a zombie? Where do zombies come from? How did they come to populate our imagination? What do they represent as modern monsters? Why the current zombie craze? Where do they (and we) go from here?

Introduction: Our Zombies, Our Remnants 5

We should note that this multi-authored project is in part the result of a symposium that we organized at SUNY-Buffalo entitled "The Zombie Phenomenon: An Interdisciplinary Conversation," where earlier (and considerably shorter) versions of this book's chapters were presented and received with great enthusiasm. Sponsored by the Cultures and Texts (C&T) Academic and Strategic Strength and the Office of the Associate Vice President for Research Advancement and Strategic Initiatives, this type of symposia encompass "research that looks critically at the world around us through building networks of researchers that weave together the perspectives and methods of multiple disciplines."[4] The particular academic and strategic strength highlighted at our symposium was "Language, Text, and Interpretation," which places special emphasis on "Aesthetics and Theory; Race and Gender; and Sexuality and Identity." This quality represents the single greatest benefit of the work presented here, as no other book has incorporated into its study of zombies such a diverse array of disciplinary and theoretical approaches.

Indeed, the authors of this volume move across and beyond the borders of established professional disciplines and fields of specialization, both individually and collectively, in order to examine the zombie phenomenon from a multitude of angles and through an array of cultural products from different periods and geographical locations, including early films like *White Zombie* (1932) and the pioneering work of Romero, as well as current shows like AMC's *The Walking Dead*, and literary offerings such as Richard Matheson's *I Am Legend* (1954) and Seth Grahame-Smith's *Pride and Prejudice and Zombies* (2009), including Spanish language narratives, from María de Zayas's seventeenth-century tale of terror *La inocencia castigada* (*Innocence Punished*) to the 2009 horror novel *Naturaleza muerta* (Dead Nature) among others.

John Edgar Browning opens the discussion with "Survival Horrors, Survival Spaces: Tracing the Modern Zombie (Cine)Myth through to the Postmillennium." Richard Matheson's canonical zombie-vampire novel, *I Am Legend* (1954), is remembered, understandably, as being among the first works of fiction to graft dystopian elements onto the vampire and zombie mythos. However, two of the novel's principal narratological features—namely, the fortified home or enclosure (i.e., the "survival space") and the crowds of infectious undead, both of which have since remained staples in nearly every subsequent zombie narrative—have gone relatively unrecognized. Browning's chapter is built on two central notions: First, the need to map out the structural principles upon which modern zombies have generally come to be defined; second, and perhaps more crucial, the need to retrace the (terato)genesis of the modern zombie cinemyth to Matheson's novel, which has been obscured or devalued over time by the work of Romero and an ever-increasing body of films and video games that have taken Romero's lead by appropriating these two essential elements of Matheson's work.

Browning's intention here is not to diminish the significance of Romero's filmic work and its impact on zombie cinema, but to urge us to recognize, rather, both Matheson's and Romero's respective configurations of the zombie mythos that have helped to institute the particular tropes with which film-makers and video game designers have embodied and continue to embody the figure of the zombie. For, as he argues, the intricacies of the *multi*-rather than *singly* defended "survival space" that Romero introduces in *Night of the Living Dead* (1968) have not only afforded the zombie subgenre its longevity but, more crucially, offer us the most compelling conceptual tool with which to trace through to the present renaissance the zombie's trajectory in popular culture and media.

Next, David Castillo takes over where Browning left off with "Zombie Masses: Monsters for the Age of Global Capitalism." His chapter re-examines the current zombie craze in the context of a discussion of modern monsters. From abnormal births to witches and vampires, to today's zombie masses, monsters have populated our imagination since the dawn of modernity. Going back to the late middle ages and the early modern period, monsters have been interpreted as both *signs* and *warnings*, in accordance with etymologies that traced the word "monster" to the Latin verbs *monstrare* (to show or reveal) and *monere* (to warn or admonish).

Taking this notion as a point of departure, this chapter asks the following questions: Why is it that our favorite monsters today are undead humans, i.e., vampires and, especially, zombies? What do our zombie narratives reveal about ourselves? What do they warn us against? Taking seriously one of the most famous lines in film zombie history, "They are us," from Romero's *Dawn of the Dead* (1978), Castillo concludes that the zombie masses are us in more ways than one: they are our dark mirror image, our sweat shops, our garbage, our landfills, our pollution, the face of globalization, an infinitely reproducible and exportable product of the mass-culture industry, and also, paradoxically, a built-in site of contestation against this same phenomenon.

Introduction: Our Zombies, Our Remnants   7

In "The Coming Apocalypses of Zombies and Globalization," David A. Reilly acknowledges the zombie subgenre's explosion into pop culture. But what is the attraction, he asks? What do zombies represent and why have they captured our interest? This chapter explores some of the answers and offers a novel hypothesis: in both the zombie apocalypse and the destructive path of globalization, individuals are empowered as states fail. Globalization has been described as a "coming anarchy" of fragmentation and homogenization that creates a sense of despair and powerlessness not unlike the onslaught of zombie hordes. Despite this, through an analysis of the diffusion process of zombification, Reilly argues that the common theme in both globalization and zombification is that the individual is empowered as the state collapses.

We can identify the parallels between the zombie and globalization apocalypses that result in a state of nature. Within, the individual has the ability to take charge of his own survival and to make choices that only s/he is accountable for. This is, as Reilly notes, the major attraction of post-apocalyptic narratives and indeed the basis of our fascination with the zombie apocalypse.

Finally, David Schmid concludes the volume with "The Limits of Zombies: Monsters for a Neoliberal Age." His chapter looks into what our monsters might most accurately represent in the current age of global neoliberalism. Although the ravenous hunger and destructiveness of zombies capture aspects of the brutal rapacity of contemporary capitalism, Schmid notes that many recent theoretical appropriations of the figure of the zombie are either opportunistic or overly simplistic in the way they read the zombie crowd as a symptom of the evils of the neoliberal world order. Moreover, the usefulness of the zombie *topos* as a way to describe or analyze our historical moment is, Schmid argues, limited by what he calls the excessive visibility of this figure; in other words, the instantaneous visual impression made by the zombies that have flooded our popular culture obscures the fact that the true monsters of neoliberalism hide in plain sight by means of their bland normality.

The chapter concludes with the suggestion that the *psychopath*, rather than the zombie, is the figure that captures most completely the ways in which both individuals and organizations operate in the neoliberal age. If we keep our focus on the corporate boardroom rather than the post-apocalyptic landscape of zombie movies, Schmid suggests, we will see the need to conceive of monstrosity not only as a symptom but also as a highly mobile, endlessly mutating, and extremely specific set of discourses, technologies, and ideologies, able to both adjust to local circumstances with great rapidity and abject (that is, render monstrous) anyone and anything that forms a barrier to capital accumulation. In this way, we will be able to bring the monsters of neoliberalism into focus and subject them to sustained scrutiny.

The incredible advances seen in Zombie Studies in the last decade are still being measured. The field is exploding with new book titles and articles that examine the zombie trope from every conceivable angle. These new studies will presumably have lasting effects on not only this cultural field but related disciplines as well. We are indeed living a zombie renaissance, vampires notwithstanding. Overall, the response from scholars, aficionados, and fans to the barrage of films, television shows, graphic novels, video games, and even zombie walks has been overwhelmingly positive. Surely, then, the present time offers an opportunity to examine the zombie phenomenon in context, and we here take advantage of this moment by doing just that while incorporating, simultaneously, a good number of recent studies and popular works of literary and cinematic fiction.

Notes

1. Richard K. Sherwin, *Visualizing Law in the Age of the Digital Baroque: Arabesques & Entanglements* (New York: Routledge, 2011), 23.
2. Ibid., 171.
3. Evgeny Morozov, "The Perils of Perfection," *New York Times*, March 2, 2013, http://www.nytimes.com/2013/03/03/opinion/sunday/the-perils-of-perfection.html?_r=1.
4. See "Cultures and Texts (C&T)," *UB 2020: University at Buffalo's Strategic Plan*, accessed November 10, 2015, https://www.buffalo.edu/ub2020/strengths/our_academic_strategicstrengths/culture.html.

1
Survival Horrors, Survival Spaces: Tracing the Modern Zombie (Cine)Myth through to the Postmillennium

John Edgar Browning

Abstract: *Crucial to this chapter is the need to resituate the (terato)genesis of the modern zombie cinemyth to Richard Matheson's* I Am Legend *(1954), which has been obscured or devalued over time by the work of George A. Romero and an ever-increasing body of films and video games that, like Romero's films, have appropriated essential elements from Matheson's work, like the "survival space." The contention here is not to diminish the significance of Romero's filmic work and its impact on zombie cinema, but to recognize, rather, both Matheson's and Romero's respective configurations of the zombie mythos that have afforded the zombie subgenre its longevity and, more crucially, offer us the most compelling conceptual tool with which to trace through to the postmillennium the zombie's trajectory in popular culture and media.*

Castillo, David R., David Schmid, David A. Reilly and John Edgar Browning. *Zombie Talk: Culture, History, Politics.* New York: Palgrave Macmillan, 2016.
DOI: 10.1057/9781137567727.0005.

Introduction: of vampires and revenants

Of the particular vampire fiction that has, in the last 60 years, crossed over into film and subsequently *redefined* the vampire subgenre[1]—that is to say, *dismantled* its "inherited conventions of the particular filmic kind in order to display [its] formal and ideological complexity, but also in order to put them back together, so to speak, in better working condition than before," to borrow from Carl Freedman's analysis[2] of the works of Stanly Kubrick—none in this category has achieved greater distinction perhaps than Richard Matheson's 1954 vampire novel *I Am Legend*.[3] The novel's first years alone saw at least four editions, from Fawcett (New York), Buccaneer (Cutchogue, NY), Nelson Doubleday (Garden City, NY), and Walker (New York), and the next five years would bring the novel's first international editions, with *Je suis une légende* (Paris: Denoël, 1955), translated by Claude Elsen; *I Am Legend* (London: Transworld, 1956); and *Soy leyenda* (Buenos Aires: Minotauro, 1960). In hindsight, these early years merely foreshadow the novel's resilience, which has scarcely diminished after at least 65 editions and 15 international translations.

Breaking from the long tradition of vampire fiction before the 1950s, Matheson's novel, to borrow again from Freedman, "offers a critical reflection on its respective generic framework, working to lay bare the absolute presuppositions of the latter—while at the same time *also* exemplifying its genre with rare brilliance."[4] More precisely, Matheson's vampires diffuse from their literary foreparents: figures "derived from folklore but now bearing precious little resemblance to them," as observed by Paul Barber.[5] The vampires of Matheson's text resemble rather the relatively older, pre-literary revenant, the peasantry's vampire. Hailing from some distant land far removed from the civilized capitals of Europe, the revenant is typically a local villager who returns from the dead to attack his family and neighbors. In this regard, *I Am Legend* (hereafter *IAL*) comes to us much in the same vein as the "proto-strain" of zombie films preceding the novel, famously with *White Zombie* (1932). The zombie of the proto-strain, like its Eastern European cousin the revenant, is generally portrayed as a distant, geographically isolated, and relatively surmountable (i.e., "single") threat. Matheson's zombie-vampires (vampire-zombies?), on the other hand, diverge from this earlier conception, helping to birth what would eventually become an entirely new breed of zombie.

Prompting this study are two things. First is the need to map out the structural *principia* upon which modern zombies have generally come to be defined. Second, and perhaps more crucial, is the need to resituate the (terato)genesis of the modern zombie cinemyth to Matheson's novel, which has been obscured or devalued over time by the work of George A. Romero and an ever-increasing body of films and video games that has followed in the wake of Romero's films. My contention, however, is not to diminish the significance of Romero's filmic work and its impact on zombie cinema. Rather, I wish to recognize both Matheson's and Romero's respective configurations of the zombie mythos that have helped to institute, in distinct but overlapping ways, the particular tropes with which film-makers and video game designers continue to embody zombies. The present study shall consider these tropes, while offering an account of their narrative complexity and continuous hybridization by other, more non-traditional, genres and narrative forms. An intersectional analysis of earlier zombie films with the more recent ones is therefore instructive for understanding not only the function of these narratives within a general zombie discourse, but also the historicity underlying the most recent string of iterations: video games. Before proceeding, however, an overview of Matheson's novel and a brief outline of the zombie's filmic progeny and its particular strains are essential.

Beginnings and bloodlines

To begin, while Matheson's text is among the first works of fiction to graft the vampire and zombie mythos with dystopian elements, its principal narratological features have gone relatively unnoted. Specifically, the novel's greatest achievements lie in the way (1) it forever infuses the figure of the zombie with mob-like tendencies; after *IAL*, the zombie would no longer be understood in mere singular terms, but would instead comprise an insurmountable force—or "multiple threat," a term I shall reiterate later. Moreover, (2) because the central "threat" in the story is re-centered *around* the Gothic edifice or enclosure (in this case, a house), rather than *inside* it, the setting depicted in Matheson's novel is an inversion of typical Gothic space and geography. As a result of this viable combination, *IAL* and its male protagonist, "Robert Neville," reaped the success of a three-film cycle over the next half a century, starting[6] with American International Pictures's *The Last Man on Earth* (1964),[7] starring

Vincent Price as "Robert Morgan." Later, two films would follow from Warner Brothers: *The Omega Man* (1971), starring Charlton Heston as "Robert Neville," and more recently *I Am Legend* (2007), this time with Will Smith in the lead role. This cycle of "straight" filmic adaptations (hereafter referred to as the "first strain") attests to the novel's enduring "generic framework," as Freedman puts it. Even more strikingly, the teratological qualities that help to distinguish Matheson's zombie are less foreign in nature than recognizably domestic. Namely, the novel firmly de-orientalizes the figure of the zombie by relocating it from its previously exotic locale, to the western spheres of suburbia and civilization, what Bernice M. Murphy describes as the genre's latest "valid gothic site."[8] It is here that the zombie and the pronouncedly anglicized bodies and faces of families, friends, and neighbors are forever after merged.

By the late 1960s, however, Matheson's novel would engender a vastly larger "second strain" comprised mainly of filmic offshoots. This body of films is, by comparison, culturally and socio-politically more prolific than what we see evidenced in the "straight" filmic adaptations of the first strain. To adequately address this second strain, I turn to Caroline J. S. Picart,[9] who similarly argues that R. J. Berenstein's description of the struggle between ideologically conservative and progressive elements in classic horror "is actually more visible in hybrid genre offshoots (as opposed to the classic or 'straight' horror versions) of the Frankensteinian narrative, as in *Alien Resurrection*."[10] In line with Picart's analysis, I approach the filmic progeny of the second strain along a similar course: that "The 'meaning' of the[se] film[s] resists being fixed by 'one' reading but reveals these various forces at work."[11]

In what follows, I will situate Romero's *Night of the Living Dead* (1968) (hereafter *NLD*) and sequel *Dawn of the Dead* (1978) (hereafter *Dawn*) as zombie films proper, the *locus classicus* of the second strain. These films, I would argue, are consistent with Freedman's postulation concerning similar horror films, in that they too provide "a rich theoretical meditation on the (much undertheorized) genre of horror itself, suggesting the historical function and ideological limits of horror as well as the complex involvement of horror with the whole category of historicity."[12] Furthermore, evidence for both Picart's and Freedman's respective claims lies visibly across the second strain, which signals a body of films that is consistent with, yet has mutated considerably from, Matheson's original narrative. While previous scholarship has examined, in considerable depth, the highly lucrative business end of Romero's low-budget reconfiguration of the zombie archetype with *NLD*, as well as its impact on subsequent zombie pictures in the second strain, this study shall focus primarily on teratogenic and narratological concerns.

The second strain has consistently preserved two essential Mathesonian elements that have remained staples in nearly every subsequent zombie narrative for the last half century. It is my contention that the preservation of these elements has allowed the second strain to continue to speak to us through its numerous cinematic retellings. The first of these elements is what I have come to call Matheson's threat en masse,[13] also familiarly known as the "multiple threat." The latter term is Gregory A. Waller's, whose influential work[14] is by necessity returned to again and again throughout this chapter, in particular because, arguably, it laid the initial groundwork for structurally based readings of zombie narratives. Similarly, on the fantastic biologies of monsters, Noël Carroll makes a similar point in his discussion of "massification,"[15] that is to say, augmenting, or *massing*, the threat phobic objects pose. The second, and least recognized, of these elements is what I shall refer to as the "survival space": the edifice or enclosure in *IAL* in which Neville—the world's only survivor—is forced to defend, fortify, and survive. However, the "survival space" in *NLD* is one in which more than one survivor simultaneously occupies and defends against the "multiple threat." Thus, the result is a more socially and politically volatile enclosure (in stark contrast to Neville's *singly* defended "survival space" in the first strain). Despite their origination, these particular features leave us with a key issue that continues to be overlooked or remain unacknowledged.

Many tend to credit these essential elements to the work of Romero. A recent example of this oversight can be found in the critically important work of Kim Paffenroth. Concerning the zombie's cinematic beginnings, Paffenroth writes, "When one speaks of zombie movies today, one is really speaking of movies that are either made by or directly influenced by George A. Romero."[16] Paffenroth goes on to say that "Romero's landmark film, *Night of the Living Dead* (1968), has defined the zombie genre since its release."[17] However, the significant elements to which Paffenroth is here alluding—the indiscriminate and voracious nature of the zombie's hunger, coupled with its advanced decompositional state; the multiplicity and insurmountability by which it threatens humanity; and the "survival space," whose occupants must, together, fortify in order to protect the enclosure from what is "outside," coping all the while with the bleak sense of disparity and hopelessness around them—are distinctly Matheson's.

On the other hand, what *is* unquestionably Romero's, as Paffenroth aptly illustrates, is the enduring pliability Romero imparts to the genre with the second strain, by reconfiguring the "survival space" into a repository for socially turbulent—and predominantly anti-capitalist—configurations, conservative and progressive negotiation, and hierarchical discourses concerning class, race, and gender. While some critics have pointed out that the zombie en masse did indeed begin with Matheson, it is scarcely acknowledged that the "survival space" is also his conception, perhaps because critics rarely treat the predominantly monolithic construction of the "survival space" in the first strain.

Thus, the question I take up below is a simple one. Stated briefly: What do Matheson's "survival space" and infectious, zombie-producing pandemic owe then to Romero's anti-capitalist (re)configurations of the "survival space" in *NLD* and *Dawn*? It seems to me, and this shall be the chief position of this article, that the intricacies of the *multi-* rather than *singly* defended "survival space" introduced in *NLD* have not only afforded the second strain its longevity, but more crucially, offer us the most compelling conceptual tool with which to trace through to the present day the trajectory of the second strain, anticipating, in its design, according to Tony Williams, "Romero's later attacks on the government/military/media, and scientific establishments."[18] By this, I am offering that the "survival space" has continuously lent the second strain its most fundamentally entertaining and dramatic qualities, permitting it to function as a highly porous "public performance space," one in which political tensioning has swelled and contracted in every sequel, adaptation, and hybridization of the zombie films I have observed since Romero's *NLD* and *Dawn*.[19] Picart identifies "cinemyths" as "public performance spaces within which patriarchal and matriarchal myths compete with each other, and where conservative and progressive ideological forces struggle against each other in working through collective anxieties, traumas, or aspirations."[20] In line with Picart's model, Ted E. Tollefson offers that "Films may be an ideal medium for generating myths that map the rapidly shifting landscape of the twentieth century," producing in the process what become "cinemyths," which for Tollefson "always bear the stamp of a particular time, place, and culture."[21]

Later, the second strain's porosity and versatility would incite crosspollinations between the film and the video gaming industries as well. Thus, "survival horror" video game titles are, for our purposes here, particularly beneficial to outlining the second strain and therefore call for examination. However, because the socio-historical development of the "survival space" is a complex one, an examination of its interiority is an equally complex endeavor. It is for this reason that I find a Marxist reading particularly useful as an interpretative tool, though to provide a balanced view its use shall be primarily one of synthesis with other scholarly works that treat the zombie's structural and representational development. It is not my goal here to provide totalizing remarks about the political landscape of the second strain. Rather, this study hopes to reveal the rich history of dialog between these texts. Thus have I drawn necessarily from previous Marxist scholarship, while relying heavily on production and distribution history, reception history, and print culture to help elucidate the zombie subgenre's complex inner workings.

Reconfiguring the "Survival Space" in NLD[22]

The topic of this section draws heavily from Waller's investigation into the distinct personalities of undead narratives, particularly *NLD*, which necessitates a brief review of Waller's main points before I may adequately extend some of them. Waller begins by noting the variant, and repetitive, representations of the undead in the nineteenth century, which he uses to "chart the ways the creatures speak to our understanding and fear of...slavish dependence and masterful control."[23] While it remains crucial, Waller explains, to position the undead's varying representations in relation "to other representations of the monstrous threat—as a single creature (like Freud's image of the primal father) or as an overwhelming mass (like certain images of the mob)," the undead's most central relation is to the "human beings these creatures stalk, feed on, and struggle against.... [T]he undead betray their origins and remain recognizably *human* [emphasis added]."[24] The inference Waller makes here is particularly germane to the slow-moving, consumptive, unceasing zombie figure Matheson's novel and Romero's films help to solidify. Steven Shaviro aptly remarks that "Romero's zombies seem almost natural in a society in which the material comforts of the middle class coexist with repressive conformism, [and] mind-numbing media manipulation."[25] In line with Waller's and Shaviro' respective claims, Slavoj Žižek concurs that "we all *are* zombies who are not aware of it, who are self-deceived into perceiving themselves as self-aware."[26] Shaviro further adds,

> The life-in-death of the zombie is a nearly perfect allegory for the inner logic of capitalism, whether this be taken in the sense of the exploitation of living labor by dead labor, the deathlike regimentation of factories and other social spaces, or the artificial, externally driven stimulation of consumers.[27]

Waller places considerable importance on the precise ways in which normalcy is represented in the home, the city, the shopping mall, etc., once these loci have been rendered safe again by the survival group. For it is this image, Waller maintains, that often "defines what is most important in and to the world."[28] It follows then that the reinstatement of the survivors' materialistic values in *NLD* underscores this observation. Thus, of the monster's origin, Waller asks, "Is the threat truly exterior to us and our world, or is the image of the monster as invader a convenient way of displacing from inside to outside?"[29] To help answer this, Waller asserts that the most common thread binding these narratives is "the threat posed by the undead and the *defensive and retaliatory action* undertaken by the living [emphasis added]," demonstrating humankind's capabilities as well as its weaknesses.[30]

Although the grand climactic confrontation between zombie and human occurs at or near the close of *IAL*, *NLD*, *Dawn*, and Romero's third installment *Day of the Dead* (1985, hereafter *Day*), which spatial constraints do not allow me to explore further, the "survival space" is itself continuously "varied and challenged by Matheson and Romero" throughout these narratives.[31] Waller is apt to explore, and do so at great length, the "role of resolution" in these narratives and resolution's ideological and psychological parameters. The interrelationship between the "destruction of the undead," the "resumption of normality," and the "concluding sequences" to these horror narratives warrant our consideration, even (or especially) in instances in which the resolution "question[s] whether normality is worth saving or resuming—assuming that it could be saved or resumed, which in these films seems unlikely, if not impossible."[32] In Romero's filmic narratives, capitalism and privatization appear equally as monstrous as the threat itself, so much so that what is inside the "survival space" and outside of it become at times indistinguishable. This breed of resolution, which "is by 1979 a conventionalized lack of finality," offers a dramatically different portrayal of the undead's survival, "as well as in its suggestions about the role of the viewer in the movement towards closure."³³ Similarly instructive are Carroll's comments on human emotional responses to horror narratives for analyzing the socio-politics of Romero's anti-capitalist zombie narratives (which I will examine in detail momentarily):

> [W]e model our emotional responses upon ones like that of the young woman [Barbra] in *Night of the Living Dead* who, when surrounded by zombies, screams and clutches herself in such a way as to avoid contact with the contaminated flesh. The characters of works of horror exemplify for us the way in which to react to the monsters of the fiction. Our emotions are supposed to mirror those of the positive human characters.³⁴

While the analogy Carroll draws between our own emotional responses as spectators and "those of the positive human characters" is an insightful one, it is clear that he makes an assumption about the political intentions of the writer and director. (*NLD*, for example, was no pawn of the studios, and was therefore not encoded with the same mores and ideologically conservative politics typical of major studio productions.) Kevin Heffernan observes that the film's "absence of stars and ... marginal place in the network of 1968 horror-film production and distribution led the film-makers to seek a particular type of product differentiation that emphasized graphic violence, bleak social commentary, and a downbeat ending."³⁵ How then, I wonder, might Carroll's analysis account for the "survival spaces" we observe in Romero's zombie narratives, ones in which the characters, although equipped with no other logical means of survival but to defend and provide for one another, instead prove self-destructive by attempting to re-privatize the shelter around them? Carroll continues:

> That the audience's emotional response is modeled on that of characters provides us with a useful methodological advantage in analyzing the emotion of art-horror. It suggests a way in which we can formulate an objective, as opposed to an introspective, picture of the emotion of horror. That is, rather than characterize art-horror solely on the basis of our subjective responses, we can ground our conjectures on observations of the way in which characters respond to monsters in works of horror.³⁶

It is perhaps for this reason that the horror of Romero's zombie films, as well as the filmic and gaming progeny these films have engendered and continue to engender, has generally proven to be meta-political. That is, rather than offer the normative (i.e., mainstream) organizational politic through which victory is attainable (i.e., American "individualism"), instead communal action is given as a safe, viable alternative. Ultimately, it too fails when the mainstream organizational politic is reinstated. Where then, I wonder, does the separation occur between survivalist and zombie, between survivalist and audience—between zombie and audience? Thus, the "survival space" calls into question simultaneously the social and economic systems upon which America functions, as well as our own initiative to resist these systems.

For Waller, it seems that "At times—as in *I Am Legend*, for example, or *Night of the Living Dead*—the work of the undead is merely the monotonous fulfillment of basic biological need."[37] Theirs is the work of consumption: ceaseless and instinctual. Therefore, "the living must also work—to challenge, mutilate, and destroy...to defend themselves, to survive, to protect, and even perhaps to redeem that which they deem most valuable in the world," using survival methods reminiscent of "what Van Helsing calls the 'wild work' of destruction.... Just as the stumbling, zombie-like creatures in *I Am Legend*" or in *NLD* and its progeny "are vastly different from the commanding, cosmopolitan Count Draculas of Bela Lugosi and Christopher Lee, so too the rough and terrible methods employed by the living vary from text to text."[38] In short, theirs is the work of survival. Waller further adds that

> all of the stories since *Dracula* can be seen in part as implicit commentaries on what C. Wright Mills...has characterized as the "conditions of modern work".... [I]n most cases the work of both the living and the undead is not an alienating, dissatisfying, economic necessity.... Here work is life, and the living are given the opportunity to take meaningful action that will determine their own destiny.[39]

I contend, however, that it is the "method" in which survival is undertaken that calls for further scrutiny. For Waller could not have imagined, in the mid-1980s, the tenacity with which the second strain would survive and multiply, nor could he have anticipated Romero's anti-capitalist leitmotif surviving alongside it.

Of the revisionist stance Romero takes towards the horror genre in general, and capitalism in particular, Waller comments that, like Murnau's and Herzog's *Nosferatu* (1922 and 1979, respectively), Romero's *NLD* questions "the price that must be paid for the survival of the bourgeois city and question[s] also the values and institutions upon which such cities are based."[40] It is within such narratives that we encounter the "multiple threat," a crucial component in many horror stories of the living and the undead after World War II. Heffernan adds to this notion, explaining that "The overt social commentary in Matheson's 1954 novel and [*The Last Man on Earth*] was part of a major component of pop-culture dystopias of the Cold War era."[41] Akin to the modern "everyday" American consumer, the zombies inspired by Matheson and Romero "lack...the vestiges of individual identity."[42] To cope with the monotony of the zombie-vampire hoard, the character of Neville in *IAL* occupies himself with the "routine of monotonous labor, [in which] life becomes 'almost bearable.'"[43] In the end, Neville's working-class ethics and individualism prove ineffective, and the hidden community of half-vampire survivors ultimately triumphs. Nevertheless, *IAL* is a necessary antecedent to Romero who introduces, extends, and enriches the notion of communal action.

On various occasions has Romero acknowledged that the original idea for *NLD* was directly inspired[44] by Matheson's novel. Matheson, too, during an interview, has commented on the striking similarities between his and Romero's work: "I remember watching television one evening decades ago and thinking to myself, 'I didn't know they filmed *I Am Legend*!' Turns out I was watching George Romero's *Night of the Living Dead*. And of course he [Romero] referred to *Living Dead* as 'homage.'"[45] An interview with Romero corroborates Matheson's suspicions. Romero explains, "The *Night of the Living Dead* thing, though, I basically ripped off from Richard Matheson's *I Am Legend*, which is really the 'Man Alone.'"[46] However, like Waller, I assert that Romero's film is a "retelling" of Matheson's novel, rather than a straightforward "reproduction." The "survival space" in *NLD*, as I noted earlier, is multiply rather than singly defended, and it is at this juncture that Waller draws comparisons between the survival group and Freud's notion of the survival/revival of Darwin's primal horde (in which a dominant patriarch exerts control over the hominid group, particularly the females[47]). On the other hand, the army of the living (un)dead is neither "an angry mob that is rioting, looting, or revolting against the status quo," nor does it "emerge from any one specific social class."[48] Instead, the zombies have been reduced, quite literally, to monotonous consumers. Thus, here lies the most illuminating parallel, which we will see as we begin to explore the fate of the survival group in more depth. Daniel C. Dennett explains that a

> zombie is or would be a human being who exhibits perfectly natural, alert, loquacious, vivacious behavior but is in fact not conscious at all, but rather some sort of automation. The whole point of the philosopher's notion of the zombie is that you can't tell a zombie from a normal person by examining

external behavior. Since that is all we ever get to see of our friends and neighbors, *some of your best friends may be zombies.*[49]

To Deleuze and Guattari, the zombies are "death instinct," which is to say that capitalism has suppressed, or "interrupted,"[50] their desires to such an extent that they have become "anti-productive": consuming without producing.

Waller descries that perhaps the "multiple threat" in Romero's film, "the 'things' that are somehow still men," are in actuality projections "of our desire to destroy, to challenge the fundamental values of America, and to bring the institutions of our modern society to a halt."[51] However, the same argument may also be extended and drawn about the survival group itself, in view of its political resonance and the "resolution" to which it ultimately succumbs. Once the survival group has been assembled under a single roof, we may observe "the fate of individual heroism, religious faith, *communal action*, romantic love, the nuclear family, and *private property*, and we can measure the fitness of man during the night of the living dead [emphasis added]."[52] Among these social institutions, it is the tension arising between the "communal action" that survival necessitates and the re-acquisition of "private property" to which the survivors are instinctually driven that eventually culminates in the demise of the band of survivors. This demise is foreshadowed intermittently as the survival group works to secure the house. Waller points out, for example, that as the character of "Ben works, [Barbra, on the other hand,] wanders through the house almost like a zombie, touching a tablecloth or a music box as if to reattach herself to some remnant of normality" and the commodities she once consumed.[53] Even Ben's behavior, as he slowly begins to privatize the materials and space around him, "can be seen as the beginning of the destruction of the ['survival space'], a piece of private property that can no longer serve as a refuge and repository of human values," and his survival is further "complicated by questions and conflicts about territoriality, authority, and responsibility."[54]

Ben issues forth his most admirable qualities in his and the house's defense against the "multiple threat," but it is the appearance of the house's other occupants that "thrusts Ben back into a social environment"[55] and, to that end, leads to his eventual demise. When confrontations begin to erupt between Harry (who hides with his wife and sick child in the basement) and Ben, the latter claims as his own domain the ground and upper floors as well as the objects contained within them. The authority Ben assumes, strengthened by the fact that he possesses the only rifle (the instrument of his pseudo-martial law over the house's other occupants), is in direct contrast with the youthful character of Tom, who serves as the representation "for the virtues of collective action.... [and] communal effort." Despite Tom's futile but heroic attempts, in the end he is unable to "forge the new community" and perishes in a truck explosion.[56] After Ben's inadequate attempts at communal action, he too ultimately fails, and the occupants of the "survival space" inevitably perish as well. However, the legacy of the communal action Tom envisioned does not end with Romero's first installment. Rather, communal action resurfaces 10 years later with the inception of the zombie-ridden mall and becomes, as a result, permanently ingrained in popular culture.

Of shopping malls and survival horrors

Romero's sequel, *Dawn*, begins with an issuance of "de-privatization" as the federal government declares martial law over zombie-infested private residences. We observe National Guard troops attempt to neutralize entire buildings infested with the living dead. Despite their tour de force, the troops incur many casualties, subsequently splintering off into individual and separate smaller groups. Like *NLD*, its sequel, *Dawn*, focuses on the efforts of a small group of survivors. In *Dawn*, the survival group is an amalgam of very different people, much in the same way it was in the first installment. Evading the chaos of Pittsburgh, a small group escapes in a helicopter, and after several hours of flight, espies an alluring sight that would become the locus of the film: a shopping mall, where hundreds of zombies have amassed. At this juncture in the film, it is less the survival group that has been dramatically reinterpreted since Romero's first installment than the "survival space" itself. Brent Adkins asks a simple but fundamentally important question: "Why is everyone at the mall?"[57] While flying overhead, one of the survival escapees asks the others, "Why do they [the zombies] come here?" The response given by another escapee is "Instinct. Memory. This was an important place in their lives." It soon becomes clear that, despite the radical alterations to the "survival space," the zombie-as-consumer motif is not only carried over from *NLD*, but is, in this case, more pronounced, even satirical.

Not surprisingly, we begin to observe the survival group orienting itself towards communal action and collectivity. Subsequently, this particular representation of survival is underscored by the fact that several "close calls" occur when individuals from the survival group behave independently; individualism spells certain death. It is only when the entire group coalesces that it is able to secure the mall, and in effect, establish it as a fortress. We soon realize, however, that the survival group has less to fear from the "multiple threat" (now contained outside the mall) than it does from the interiority of the "survival space" itself, which now threatens its communal social order. Once the shopping mall has been secured, the dangers inherent in occupying it soon become evident. As the survival group begins to settle in its new home, and as less and less communal action becomes required of them, members of the survival group resort back to the role of the consumer. They begin to live, shop, and behave lavishly, drifting idly from store to store much in the same way the zombies had. Indeed, the "recreation of 'normal' domestic life, defined here by its facile comforts and limiting roles,"[58] proves nearly fatal. For in the end, as in so many other tales of fantasy that have come before, the wealth and gold ultimately bring the dragon.

At the film's conclusion, the mall's domesticated survivors glimpse, through a glass darkly, mirror images of themselves, in the shape of a roving band of misfit, opportunistic bikers bent on pillaging whatever stands in its way. The survival group's only logical course of action here is to seek refuge in the upper levels of the mall, safely hidden from the marauders. Instead, members of the survival group begin exhibiting behavior much like Ben and Harry's in Romero's first installment—all-out brawling, gunfire, and, eventually, death—which they do not in self-defense or for survival, but in an attempt to re-privatize the mall for themselves.

After *Dawn*, Romero's zombie film cycle bears at least six additional installments, including *Day* (1985), *Night of the Living Dead* (1990), *Dawn of the Dead* (2004) (hereafter *Dawn* [2004]), *Land of the Dead* (2005) (hereafter *Land*), *Diary of the Dead* (2007), and *Survival of the Dead* (2009). The second strain is not limited to Romero's films alone, however. Romero's and Matheson's viable formula has also spawned a host of parodic offshoots, including *The Return of the Living Dead* (1985), *Return of the Living Dead Part II* (1988), *Return of the Living Dead 3* (1993), and *Return of the Living Dead 4: Necropolis* (2005); *Shaun of the Dead* (2004); even mouthfuls like *Night of the Day of the Dawn of the Son of the Bride of the Return of the Revenge of the Terror of the Attack of the Evil, Mutant, Alien, Flesh Eating, Hellbound, Zombified Living Dead Part 2: In Shocking 2-D* (1991). While in each of these titles the qualities instituted by Matheson and Romero are manifest, some later films, like the *Resident Evil* films (2002–7) and

Silent Hill (2006), are not as easily discernable because they have looked for inspiration primarily to "first-person shooter" video game titles of the "survival horror" genre, which is in itself an offshoot of the zombie franchise. Richard J. Hand, who has treated, in considerable depth, the convergence of the video gaming and horror film industries, defines the "survival horror" genre as presenting "a game in which the player leads an individual character through an uncanny narrative and hostile environment where the odds are weighed decidedly against the avatar," and in many cases, "behind the closed doors of a neo-gothic house."[59] Clearly the ways in which Romero enriched the zombie narrative have given rise to a fanbase that seeks the interactivity offered by the "survival space." On the *Resident Evil* games (1996–2015), Hand writes that

> As is true for any experience, participants—"survivors"—make sense of it by telling stories. Players of *Resident Evil* take delight in sharing anecdotes from playing the game as well as trading secrets and speculations.... It is, therefore, the experience of successfully playing the game that has created the depth and the need for the embellished universe of *Resident Evil*.[60]

Curiously, the resulting single-player (i.e., single-defender) game-play resembles more often the qualities of the *first* rather than second strain, despite the "homage" game designers claim they are paying Romero. Hand rightly points out that Romero's *NLD* offers a "liberal critique of capitalism," and that with The Umbrella Corporation of the *Resident Evil* franchise emerges "a similar sense of conspiracy and cynicism about global capitalism."[61] But, like so many others, Hand falls into the same quagmire, mistakenly ascribing to Romero's *NLD* the "zombie topos in contemporary horror film," even adding that Romero and John A. Russo's screenplay "is in many ways a straightforward reworking of *The Birds*."[62] (Ironically, Matheson was asked by Alfred Hitchcock to do a treatment for *The Birds*, but because Matheson "wanted more of an emphasis on the characters in the story, with the birds being featured less prominently," his involvement with the project was cut.[63]) However, Hand offers a redeemingly compelling critique of the *Resident Evil* games: interactive texts that he contends "incorporate distinctly cinematic points of view, which construct fixed mise en scène shots,"[64] thus making the "survival horror" genre a relatively easy one to adapt to movie screens.[65] Producers of the first *Resident Evil* (2002) initially tasked Romero with drafting a screenplay, but in the end the task of writing and directing the final product was left to Paul W. S. Anderson (who brought *Mortal Kombat* [1995] to the screen). Interestingly, where the *Resident Evil* films seem to prefer the singly defended "survival space," *Silent Hill* (another game adapted for film) seems to be a hybrid of the two, using interchangeably both single- and multi-perspective narrative spaces. This theme develops exponentially over the course of the 2000s and 2010s through an array of MMOs (massively multiplayer online games) and MMORPGs (massively multiplayer online role-playing games), in which players mobilize, cooperate, and fight zombies together over a number of network-capable platforms. However, change was in the air. Although the "survival space" persists in various forms in these new narrative spaces, games at this time simultaneously play host to a theme that becomes a staple of post-millennial zombie narratives—ambulation, which I cover at length in the next section.

The juxtaposition of filmic and video game conventions that we see evidenced in the *Resident Evil* films and *Silent Hill* has culminated in a lucrative, "hybrid" formula for big studios. Paradoxically, this hybrid formula has produced a new body of work with films like *28 Days Later* (2002), *28 Weeks Later* (2007), and *Doomsday* (2008), which, in turn, have been adapted, or are being considered for adaptation, by gaming studios. Thus, Romero's (re)configuration of the "survival space," which has over time served as an economy for social and political strife, is now seeing its own circulation through a technological economy of production, one that promises to further extend and complicate the "survival space." Much like the films of the first and second strains, games of the "survival horror" genre, to borrow from Hand's analysis, "create dream houses for contemporary collectives, places where players enter the thrills of the labyrinth and return with solutions and stories," a world that "abounds with variation, homage, and folklore, all of which surrounds the core 'myth' and provides a fascinating insight into a broad cross-section of contemporary popular culture."[66]

Surviving the post-millennial zombie

The new millennium has introduced marked changes in zombie cinema, in particular or especially the viability of the "survival space" itself. In fact, what we have seen since 2001 are either fewer or largely unsustained "survival spaces" and a pronounced trend towards what I am calling "ambulatory survival spaces": groups behaving more nomadically, setting out across no small distance from space to space. Perhaps the earliest attempt at ambulation, even if a failed one, occurs in Romero's *NLD* with the survival group's disastrous attempt to appropriate the farmhouse's gasoline pump. Afterwards, Romero's *Dawn* and *Day* also feature ambulation, this time by way of helicopter, though in both instances the decision is more or less reactionary to some immediate danger transpiring in the film's final, fleeting moments and has little or no sustained narratological significance. Perhaps the first noteworthy example of ambulation in a second strain zombie film occurs in *Night of the Comet* (1984), only in this story the lone survivors—the last on Earth for all they know—show more in common, given their few numbers, with the solitary character of Neville from Matheson's original narrative; what is more, they have little practical need for a central "survival space" in a city only sparsely inhabited by flesh-hungry zombies. With the September 2001 attacks, however, things begin to change with the emergence of what can only be described as a distinctly third strain of zombie pictures.

The new millennium has seemingly introduced a wide-spread sense of futility to the longstanding need to create and occupy for any extended duration a central "survival space." This new trend is begat by *28 Days Later*, a film about a few survivors who take up with one another and set out in a car to find refuge at a supposed military base. Alain Silver and James Ursini assert that "rather than envision the zombie plague...as an opportunity for social commentary about racial or cultural prejudices, [Danny] Boyle," the film's director, "constructs a metaphor for basic human defects, for mankind's tendency towards violence."[67] Boyle's *28 Days Later* unveils what may be called, within a post-Romerian zombie mythos, the first real sense of survival's futility; hope has been reduced to a mere glimmer. Silver and Ursini surmise Boyle's solution to this dire scene thusly: "newly formed family ties enhanced one's survival chances,"[68] which is a utopic idea, one that, although played with in zombie cinema three decades earlier, was simply not feasible under a post-/wartime politics driven by social unrest like Romero's era. Thus, a question arises here: What prompted this new, post-millennial aesthetic in the zombie mythos?

In the documentary *Doc of the Dead* (2014), Robert Kirkman, creator/writer of the best-selling comic series *The Walking Dead* (2003–), offers a pertinent remark or two that may help to shed some light on the new zombie aesthetic: "*The Walking Dead* came about because of my love for George Romero films and zombie films in general. But these films always ended with everyone dying, or everyone but for a few survivors who ride off into the sunset—but you never know where they go."[69] Yet the trend of which Kirkman is here speaking began a year earlier with *28 Days Later* (that is, 28 days *after* the zombie pandemic has spread). Boyle's film treats of the question, "What happens next?" and Kirkman's series has quite effectively run with this notion. Yet the narratological event Boyle and Kirkman espouse, coupled with the survival group's new ambulatory impulse to *move on*, is clearly rooted in the events of 9/11.

Recent scholarship[70] has tended to examine the overt connections between post-millennial zombie cinema and the 9/11 attacks in terms of urban violence and "crisis" or apocalyptic imagery. However, although Kyle Bishop[71] dances around the topic, few or no scholars have explicitly stated that the metropolitan setting is used not only to conjure images of urban violence but has, in fact, become *the* conventional site of the majority of post-millennial zombie films following 9/11. This is prescient: the lack of public and private transportation that plagued New York City on September 11, 2001, and New Orleans after Hurricane Katrina, together with the foot traffic that ensued as a result, lends itself narratologically to the question of, "What happens next?" and the new ambulatory impulse. Both, as I have stated, are defining markers of the post-millennial strain of zombie films.

The 2004 remake of Romero's *Dawn of the Dead* emphasized vacating its "survival space" (a shopping mall) much sooner than did its original counterpart in 1978. Both *Land*, Romero's fourth installment, and the lesser-known *Doomsday* demonstrated, like *Dawn* (2004), the potential corrosiveness of a long-duration "survival space" (ibid). The roving band of survivors in *Zombieland* (2009) threw off almost entirely the need for a "survival space," while AMC's immensely popular *The Walking Dead* (2010–present) has continuously demonstrated ambulation between not one but a succession of "survival spaces" and survival groups. Not surprisingly, consumption of these new productions has inevitably fed into the zombie's increasingly multimodally rich public culture.

If survival horror video games have shown us anything, it is that zombie culture is recursive. Observe, for example, Max Brooks's wildly popular survival guide parody, *The Zombie Survival Guide: Complete Protection from the Living Dead* (2003),[72] which has practically become the field manual to post-millennial ambulation. The ambulation of survival groups, as Brooks's book demonstrates, also necessarily encourages the search for new and more effective weapons, a development which may have had unforeseen political consequences. Indeed, I have found there to be a strong parallel between recent anxieties about the prospect of new gun control laws and the influx in zombie pictures, so much so that folks who frequent zombie films seem honestly (or in jest?) to be using the notion of a "zombie apocalypse" as the premise for purchasing, and in numerous cases stockpiling, more guns and ammunition. There is no denying it: What better way to tout the need for relaxed gun laws than the possibility of a zombie apocalypse, an event during which any survivor without proper weaponry is doomed?

Zombie films and narratives are cultural artifacts with anthropological and ethnographic value, capable of showing us a great many things about ourselves in times of crisis. The walking dead are not drawing the public in any more now than they did subsequent to the release of Matheson's novel; nor is it any longer merely the cramming of a few disparate individuals into an enclosure or space and forcing them to work together in order to survive (or get killed if they do not), a formula responsible for keeping the zombie pictures fresh, interesting, and relevant for over 45 years. "What happens next," the subgenre's new mantra of ambulation, has instilled hope in a class of films where before there was little. *The Walking Dead*'s revelation that "We're all [already] infected" is seemingly contradictory to this, but perhaps hope lies in our reappraisal of the "other," of what *is* other. Perhaps it was us all along, and the new motif of ambulation, little more than our journey to self-discovery.

Conclusions

Finally, *IAL*'s print history is important to return to because it offers an alternative means by which to map out the novel's filmic strains, while illuminating simultaneously its rich social topography and international appeal. As the following bibliography[73] demonstrates, *IAL*'s iconic status—with some 64 print editions in at least fourteen different languages, including Braille—rivals even *Dracula*'s, and therefore merits our consideration:

1950s

▸ *I Am Legend: A Gold Medal Original*. Fawcett Publications: New York, 1954. 160 p. 18 cm. Series: Gold Medal Book. Cover: painting by Stan Meltzoff.

- *I Am Legend*. Walker: New York, 1954. 312 p. pbk.
- *I Am Legend*. Buccaneer Books: Cutchogue, NY, 1954. 151 p. 23 cm.
- *I Am Legend*. Nelson Doubleday: Garden City, NY, 1954. 151 p. 22 cm.
- *Je suis une legend*. Denoël (impr. de Floch): Paris, 1955. 192 p. Translation: Claude Elsen.
- *I Am Legend*. Transworld: London, 1956. 192 p. 16 cm. Series: A Corgi Book.
- *I Am Legend*. Fawcett Publications: New York, 1957. 160 p. 19 cm.

1960s

- *Soy leyenda*. Minotauro: Buenos Aires, 1960. 172 p. 20 cm. Series: Ciencia ficción. Translation: Manuel Figueroa.
- *I Am Legend*. Transworld: London, 1960. 188 p. 19 cm. Series: A Corgi Book.
- *Ich, der letzte Mensch*. Heyne: München, Germany, 1963. 152 p. Series: Heyne Bücher. Translation: Werner Gronwald.
- *I Am Legend*. Bantam Books: New York, 1964. 122 p. 18 cm.

1970s

- *I vampiri*. De Carlo: Torino, Italy, n.d. [c.1970]. 207 p. 18 cm. Series: Gamma il fantalibro. Translation: Lucia Milani. Cover: Emilio de' Rossignoli.
- *Ich, der letzte Mensch*. Heyne: München, 1970. 152 p. Series: Heyne-Bücher. Translation: Werner Gronwald.
- *I Am Legend*. Walker: New York, 1970. 122 p. 22 cm. pbk.
- *Det siste mennesket*. Fredhøis Forlag: Oslo, Norway, n.d. [c.1970]. 158 p. 18 cm. Translation: Helge Skolem.
- *The Omega Man: I Am legend*. Berkley: New York, 1971. 174 p. 18 cm. Series: A Berkley Medallion Book.
- *I Am Legend (Reissued)*. Transworld: London, 1971. 141 p. 18 cm. Series: A Corgi Book.
- *Jeg er den sidste*. Forlaget Notabene: Copenhagen, 1972. 192 p. 18 cm. Translation: Rose-Marie Tvermoes.
- *Ik ben een legende*. Bruna: Utrecht, 1972. 188 p. 18 cm. Series: Bruna science fiction. Translation: F. Lancel vertaling.
- *Jeg er den sidste*. Notabene: Copenhagen, 1972. 192 p. Translation: Peter Sugar.

Survival Horrors, Survival Spaces 29

- *Je suis une léende*. Culture, Art, Loisirs: Paris, 1973. 21 cm. illus. Translation: Claude Elsen.
- *I Am Legend*. Bruce & Watson: London, 1974. 122 p. 22 cm.
- *Varulvarnas natt*. Ryslig Midnattsläsning: Copenhagen, 1975. 158 p. 18 cm. Series: Kalla karar. Translation: Gösta Zetterlund.
- *I Am Legend*. Corgi Books: London, 1977. 141 p. 18 cm. illus.
- *I Am Legend*. Berkley: New York, 1979. 174 p. 18 cm.
- *Ja sam legenda*. Jugoslavija: Beograd, 1979. 147 p. 21 cm. Series: Biblioteka Kentaur: naucna fantastika. Translation: Zoran Zivkovic.

1980s

- *Ich bin Legende*. Heyne Verlag: München, 1982. 18 cm. illus. Series: Heyne Bücher/Bibliothek der Science Fiction Literatur. Translation: Lore Straßl. Edition: Illustrierte Sonderausg. in ugekürzter Neuübersetzung.
- *Soy leyenda*. Planeta: Barcelona, 1986. 155 p. 19 cm. Translation: Jaime Bellavista.
- *I Am Legend*. Robinson: London, 1987. 144 p. 20 cm.
- *Soy leyenda*. Minotauro: Barcelona, 1988. 179 p. 21 cm. Translation: Manuel Figueroa. Edition: 1a. ed.
- *Sóc llegenda*. Laertes: Barcelona, 1988. 154 p. 20 cm. Series: L'arcà. Translation: Carles Urritz and Carme Geronès.

1990s

- *Je suis une légende*. Denoël: Paris, 1990. 191 p. 18 cm. Series: Présence du future. Translation: Claude Elsen.
- *I Am Legend*. Buccaneer Books: Cutchogue, NY, 1991. 151 p. 23 cm.
- *Je suis une légende*. le Grand livre du mois: Paris, 1991. 191 p. 24 cm. Translation: Claude Elsen.
- *I Am Legend: Book One*. Eclipse Books: Forestville, CA, 1991. 1–60 p. 26 cm. pbk. illus. Adaptation: Steve Niles. Illustration: Elman Brown.
- *I Am Legend: Book Two*. Eclipse Books: Forestville, CA, 1991. 61–120 p. 26 cm. pbk. illus. Adaptation: Steve Niles. Illustration: Elman Brown.
- *I Am Legend: Book Three*. Eclipse Books: Forestville, CA, 1991. 121–80 p. 26 cm. pbk. illus. Adaptation: Steve Niles. Illustration: Elman Brown.
- *I Am Legend*. ORB (A Tom Doherty Associates book): New York, 1995. 317 p. 21 cm. anth.

▶ *I Am Legend.* Tom Doherty Associates: New York, 1995. 312 p. 18 cm. anth. pbk. Edition: 1st TOR.
▶ *The Paranoid Fifties: Three Classic Science Fiction Novels.* Quality Paperback Book Club: New York, 1995. 751 p. 21 cm. anth.
▶ *I Am Legend.* ORB: New York, 1997. 317 p. 21 cm. Edition: 1st ORB trade pbk. Notes: Reproduced in Braille by National Braille Association in 7 vols., 503 p./vol.
▶ *Blood Thirst: 100 Years of Vampire Fiction.* Oxford University Press: New York, 1997. 379 p. 23 cm. Compilation: Leonard Wolf.
▶ *I Am Legend.* Millennium: London, 1999. 160 p. 20 cm. Series: SF Masterworks.

2000s

▶ *Soy leyenda.* Círculo de Lectores: Barcelona, 2000. 188 p. 21 cm. Translation: Manuel Figueroa.
▶ *Gecenin konuklari.* Beyaz balina: Istanbul, 2000. 180 p. 19 cm. Series: Edebiyat/Korku. Translation: Afif Yesari.
▶ *Legenda. Rasskazy.* AST: Moskva, 2001. 541 p. 21 cm. Series: Klassika literatury uzhasov.
▶ *I Am Legend.* Gollanz: London, 2001. 160 p. 20 cm. Series: SF masterworks.
▶ *Richard Matheson's I Am Legend.* IDW Publishing: San Diego, 2003. p. 27 cm. illus. Adaption: Steve Niles and Elman Brown.
▶ *Je suis une légende.* Éd. France loisirs: Paris, 2004. 21 cm. illus. Translation: Nathalie Serval.
▶ 나는전설이다 (*Na nun chonsol ida*). Hwanggŭm Kaji: Sŏul, 2005. 427 p. 22 cm. Series: Million sello k`ullop. Translation: Yong-hak Cho.
▶ *I Am Legend* [screenplay]. 2006. 117 p. 28 cm. Adaptation: Akiva Goldsman and Mark Prostavovich.
▶ *Soy leyenda.* Minotauro: Barcelona, 2006. 179 p. 18 cm. Series: 1a. ed. en Colección Booket. Translation: Manuel Figueroa.
▶ *I Am Legend.* Gollancz: London, 2006. 161 p. 00. Series: Gollancz SF. Introduction: Stephen King.
▶ *I Am Legend.* Quality Paperback Book Club: New York, 2006. 317 p. 21 cm. anth.
▶ *Bloodlines: Richard Matheson's Dracula, I am Legend, and Other Vampire Stories.* Gauntlet Press: Colorado Springs, CO, 2006. 29 cm. anth. illus. Edition: First. Editor: Mark Dawidziak.

- *I Am Legend*. Gollancz: London, 2007. 176 p. Edition: New edition.
- *I Am Legend*. Zwarte Beertjes Uitgeverij: Utrecht, 2007. 188 p. 18 cm. pbk. Series: Pockets populaire fictie.
- *I Am Legend*. TOR: New York, 2007. 312 p. 18 cm.
- *I Am Legend*. Orion House: London, 2007.
- *I Am Legend*. TOR: New York, 2007. 312 p. 18 cm. anth. Pbk. Edition: 2nd TOR.
- *I Am Legend*. Tom Doherty Associates: New York, 2007. 320 p.
- *I Am Legend*. Gollancz: London, 2007. 161 p. 18 cm. pbk. Series: Gollancz S.F.
- *I Am Legend*. Tom Doherty Associates: New York, 2007. 317 p. 21 cm. anth. Series: 1st Tor trade paperback.
- *I Am Legend and Other Stories*. Blackstone Audiobooks: Ashland, OR, 2007. Edition/Format: Audiobook [MP3-CD].
- אני האגדה (*Ani ha-agadah*). Yanshuf: Tsur Mosheh, Israel, 2007. 192 p. 21 cm. Translation: Ya`el `Inbar.
- 我是傳奇 (*Wo shi chuan qi*). Taibei Xian Xindian Shi (台北縣新店市): Zong jing xiao Zhen de tu shu shi ye you xian gong si (總經銷楨德圖書事業有限公司), 2007. 431 p. 21 cm. Series: Storytella. Edition: Chu ban. Translation: Zongchen Chen.
- *I Am Legend*. Zwarte Beertjes: Utrecht, 2007. 188 p. 18 cm. Translation: F. Lancel.
- *I Am Legend* [audiobook on disc]. Blackstone Audio: Ashland, OR, 2007. Duration: 5:30 hours. 5 compact discs. Narration: Robertson Dean.
- *I Am Legend* [audiobook on disc]. Landmark Audiobooks: Prince Frederick, MD, 2007. Duration: 5:30 hours. 5 compact discs. Narration: Robertson Dean.
- *I Am Legend* [audiobook on tape]. Blackstone Audio: Ashland, OR, 2007. anth. 8 cassettes (83 minutes each). Narration: Robertson Dean and Yuri Rasovsky.
- *I Am Legend*. IDW Publishing: San Diego, 2007. p. 26 cm. illus. Adaptation: Steve Niles. Illustration: Elman Brown.
- *Jestem legenda*. Egmont Polska: Warszawa, 2007. 240 p. 27 cm. Illus. Series: Obrazy Grozy/Klub SK. Translation: Michal Bochenek. Adaptation: Steve Niles. Illustration: Elman Brown.
- *I Am Legend*. Orion Pub Co: London, 2008.
- *Thành phố chết*. Văn Hóa Sài Gòn: TP. Hồ Chí Minh, 2008. 221 p. 21 cm. Translation: Hương Lan.

- *Jaz sem legenda*. ZAMIK: Ljubljana, 2008. 220 p. 24 cm. Series: Zbirka Daljna obzorja. Edition: 1. izd. Translation: Teja Bivic.
- *Jestem legenda*. Wydawnictwo MAG: Warszawa, 2008. 223 p. 20 cm. Translation: Paulina Braiter.
- *Wo shi chuan qi*. Shanghai yi wen chu ban she: Shanghai, 2008. 425 p. 21 cm. Edition: Di 1 ban. Translation: Zongchen Chen.
- *Soy leyenda*. Minotauro: Mexico, 2008. 179 p. 18 cm. Series: Minotauro. Translation: Manuel Figueroa.
- Я—легенда (*IA—legenda*). EKSMO: Moskva, 2008. 459 p. 21 cm. anth. Series: Intellektual'nyi bestseller. Note: Simultaneous printing by Sankt-Peterburg: Domino.
- *Io sono leggenda*. Fanucci editore: Roma, 2008. 211 p. 23 cm. Edition: 1a ed., 2a rist. Translation: Simona Fefè. Afterword: Valerio Evangelisti.
- *CCTV乡约 : 我是传奇* = I Am Legend (*CCTV xiang yue : wo shi chuan qi = I am legend*). Beijing Shi: Dang dai Zhongguo chu ban she, 2009. 262 p. 25 cm. Translation: Xiao Dongpo.

2010s

- *Я— легенда /ĪA—legenda*. Moskva: Ėksmo, 2010. 476 p. 21 cm. Series:Kniga-zagadka, kniga-mistika. Note: Translation of *I Am Legend* and *The Incredible Shrinking Man*; simultaneous printing by Sankt-Peterburg: Domino.
- *Eu sono a lenda*. Sic Idea y Creación Editorial: Barcelona, 2010. 179 p. 22 cm. Translation: Fernando Ribeiro and David Soares.
- *Eu sou a lenda*. Sic Idea y Creación Editorial D.L.: Barcelona, 2010. 179 p. 22 cm. Translation: Fernando Ribeiro and David Soares.
- *Je suis une légende*. Éd. France loisirs: Paris, 2013. 975 p. 20 cm. Translation: Nathalie Serval. Note: Includes translations of *Bid Time Return* (trans. Ronald Blunden) and *The Incredible Shrinking Man* (trans. Jacques Chambon).
- *Par-delà la légende: romans*. Denoël: Paris, 2014. 734 p. 19 cm. Translation: Nathalie Serval. Note: Includes translations of *Bid Time Return* (trans. Ronald Blunden) and *The Incredible Shrinking Man* (trans. Jacques Chambon).
- *I Am Legend and Other Stories* [eAudiobook]. Blackstone Audio, Inc.: Ashland, 2015. Duration: 10:52 hours. Online resource. Narration: Robertson Dean and Yuri Rasovsky.

IAL's print history, showing particular fluctuations just prior to and following the release of first- and second-strain films and video games, underscores the intertextuality between Matheson's and Romero's progeny. Moreover, the assimilation of Matheson's text by alternative narrative forms (such as graphic novels, audiobooks, and video games), and the strength of its international appeal outside of predominantly Anglocentric markets during the late 2000s, suggests that the novel and its hybrid offspring have continued to maintain with some regularity a place in popular media.

To conclude my analysis, I find it important to review some of the major threads of my discussion. Ultimately, I have examined, and attempted to extend, the relationship others before me have drawn between the zombie-producing pandemic of Matheson's novel and the zombie filmic narratives that occur after the novel, particularly those by Romero beginning with *NLD* in 1968. In my analysis of Matheson's and Romero's works, I have attempted to show that the parallels between Matheson's novel and its representative filmic adaptations and offshoots have not been restricted to Waller's notion of the "multiple threat." Rather, I have argued that there are other, equally important, parallels that must be drawn between the novel and the films, particularly the notion of a "survival space." In order to address these areas, I first examined what I refer to as the "proto-strain" of zombie films (i.e., pre-Matheson). I then proceeded to show how it is important, in the zombie's cinematic history, to remind ourselves that Matheson's novel re-envisaged the proto-strain by establishing what would become the subgenre's canonical markers, one involving what Carroll refers to as "massification," and the other involving a centrally defended enclosure (which I shall discuss below in more detail). From there, I distinguished and elaborated on what I inferred to be two distinct Matheson-inspired "strains" of zombie films: the first strain, or "novelistic adaptations" (i.e., single survivor); and the second strain, or "novelistic offshoots" (i.e., multiple survivor). More precisely, it is the second strain that has dominated zombie films for the last 40 years. It is also here where I drew two fundamental arguments.

First and foremost, I argued that an equally striking parallel could be drawn linking Matheson's novel to the second strain beyond the mere presence of the infectious zombie-producing pandemic, a quality to which this strain of films is typically reduced. Rather, in addition to the zombie-producing pandemic and "multiple threat" (again, applying Waller's term), Matheson's novel sets forth a sort of reactionary "survival space," in which "the one" (or "few") defends an enclosure against "the many." Indeed, it is this "survival space" that has lent the novel in general, and the filmic progeny of the second strain in particular, its most fundamentally entertaining and dramatic qualities. In sum, Matheson and Romero have imparted to us a highly porous "performance space," one in which political tensioning and negotiation have continuously swelled and contracted in nearly every sequel, adaptation, and hybridization of the zombie film since Romero's 1968 classic. Therefore, it is both Matheson's infectious zombie-producing pandemic and the inception of the "survival space," and the socio-historical rhythms to which it has played host, that we owe our modern conception of the zombie narrative.

In both filmic strains, capitalist culture is crippled under the strain of the zombie upheaval. However, in the second strain, we see the formulation of communally organized groups. Generally inhabiting an enclosure in which the collective efforts of the entire group are needed to sustain life, these communal groups are drawn into self-destruction, typically after one or more of the group's members attempts to re-privatize the enclosure, an event, I argue, that has continued to manifest, in some variation, in the second strain. I further add that this tendency towards re-privatization reveals our close proximity to zombies and their behavior as mindless consumers, on which even Žižek has commented, saying that "we all *are* zombies who are not aware of it, who are self-deceived into perceiving themselves as self-aware."[74] As Fran (the only female member of the survival group in *Dawn*) asks, once the group has secured the shopping mall, "Who the hell are they [the zombies]?" To which Peter, the black hero, responds, "They're us, that's all."

Central to the notion of which Fran and Peter speak is the chapter's final section, wherein I attempt to elucidate the post-millennial reworking of the zombie that has subsequently given rise to what is, arguably, an entirely new third strain, one comprised predominantly of nomadic or ambulatory survival practices and spaces. However, this raises the current zombie cycle's most critical point of context. Namely, what are the survivalists searching for amid such devastation and struggle—*life*? Or is it *hope*? Perhaps it is this pursuit, more than any other, which lends the current zombie renaissance its best quality: Where before there was little, or none, humanity is finding hope in increasing abundance.

Notes

I would like to thank Intellect Ltd. for permission to publish this expanded version of my previous essay. I am also indebted to a number of my students at the Georgia Institute of Technology, who through class discussion and one-on-one conversation helped me at times to flesh out and articulate more clearly the topic of zombies in post-millennial films and video games.

1. This event, as the present chapter sets out to show, anticipates Gilles Deleuze and Félix Guattari's observation that "the only modern myth is the myth of zombies." Gilles Deleuze and Félix Guattari, *A Thousand Plateaus: Capitalism and Schizophrenia* (Minneapolis: University of Minnesota Press, 1987), 335.
2. Carl Freedman, *The Incomplete Projects: Marxism, Modernity, and the Politics of Culture* (Middletown, CT: Wesleyan University Press, 2002), 91.
3. Matheson's novel is, in this respect, closely followed by Anne Rice's 1976 novel *Interview with the Vampire*, and by Bram Stoker's *Dracula* almost 80 years earlier.
4. Freedman, *The Incomplete Projects*, 91.
5. Paul Barber, *Vampires, Burial, and Death: Folklore and Reality* (New Haven, CT: Yale University Press, 1988) 2.
6. Vampire scholar J. Gordon Melton notes that Matheson was initially hired by Hammer Films as early as the late 1950s to begin work on a film treatment after the studio purchased the rights to the novel. However, Hammer stopped production after the British censor's office threatened a total ban in England. J. Gordon Melton, *The Vampire Book: The Encyclopedia of the Undead* (Canton, MI: Visible Ink Press, 1998), 322.
7. Matheson was reputedly so dissatisfied with the co-adapted script for American International Pictures's film version, *The Last Man on Earth*, that he credited himself as "Logan Swanson." See Melton (1998), and *The Internet Movie Database (IMDb)*.
8. Bernice M. Murphy, *The Suburban Gothic in American Popular Culture* (Hampshire, UK: Palgrave Macmillan, 2009), 15.
9. Caroline J. S. Picart, "The Third Shadow and Hybrid Genres: Horror, Humor, Gender and Race in Alien Resurrection," *Communication and Critical/Cultural Studies* 1, no. 4. (2004): 336–7.
10. R. J. Berenstein, *Attack of the Leading Ladies: Gender, Sexuality, and Spectatorship in Classic Horror Cinema* (New York: Columbia University Press, 1996), 10.
11. Picart, "The Third Shadow and Hybrid Genres," 336–7.
12. Freedman, *The Incomplete Projects*, 91.
13. As observed by Richard J. Hand, "Proliferating Horrors: Survival Horror and the *Resident Evil* Franchise," in *Horror Film: Creating and Marketing Fear*, ed. Steffen Hantke (Jackson, MS: University Press of Mississippi, 2009), 129, films like Alfred Hitchcock's *The Birds* (1963), which pre-dates the first

strain, have treated the en masse theme. However, it is worth noting that Hitchcock's avian threat is non-humanoid and geographically isolated.
14 Gregory A. Waller, *The Living and the Undead: From Stoker's Dracula to Romero's Dawn of the Dead* (Urbana, IL: University of Illinois Press, 1986).
15 Noël Carroll, *The Philosophy of Horror: Or, Paradoxes of the Heart* (New York: Routledge, 1990), 50.
16 Kim Paffenroth, *Gospel of the Living Dead: George Romero's Visions of Hell on Earth* (Waco, TX: Baylor University Press, 2006), 1.
17 Ibid.
18 Tony Williams, *The Cinema of George Romero: Knight of the Living Dead* (London: Wallflower Press, 2003) 29.
19 Picart, "The Third Shadow and Hybrid Genres," 335.
20 Ibid., 334–5.
21 Ted E. Tollefson, "Cinemyths: Contemporary Films as Gender Myth," in *Soul of Popular Culture: Looking at Contemporary Heroes, Myths, and Monsters*, ed. Lynn Kittelson (Peru, IL: Open Court, 1998), 107–8.
22 This section takes Steven Shaviro's remarks on Romero as a thematic premise: "Romero is at once the pornographer, the anthropologist, the allegorist, and the radical critic of contemporary American culture. He gleefully uncovers the hidden structures of our society in the course of charting the progress of its disintegration." Steven Shaviro, *The Cinematic Body* (Minneapolis: University of Minnesota Press, 1993), 82.
23 Waller, *The Living and the Undead*, 16.
24 Ibid.
25 Shaviro, *The Cinematic Body*, 83.
26 Slavoj Žižek, *Organs Without Bodies: On Deleuze and Consequences* (New York: Routledge, 2004), 136.
27 Shaviro, *The Cinematic Body*, 83.
28 Waller, *The Living and the Undead*, 17.
29 Ibid.
30 Ibid., 18.
31 Ibid., 18–19.
32 Ibid., 19.
33 Ibid., 20.
34 Noël Carroll, "The Nature of Horror," *The Journal of Art Aesthetics and Art Criticism* 46, no. 1 (1987): 53.
35 Kevin Heffernan, "Inner-City Exhibition and the Genre Film: Distributing Night of the Living Dead (1968)," *Cinema Journal* 41, no. 3 (2002): 66.
36 Carroll, "The Nature of Horror," 53.
37 Waller, *The Living and the Undead*, 20.
38 Ibid., 20–1.
39 Ibid., 22–3.

40 Ibid., 225.
41 Heffernan, "Inner-City Exhibition and the Genre Film," 69.
42 Waller, *The Living and the Undead*, 256.
43 Ibid., 260.
44 See also George A. Romero, (1974), preface to *Night of the Living Dead*, by John Russo (New York: Warner Books, 1974), 10; and Mike Wilmington and Barry Brown, "Interview: George Romero, Knight of the Living Dead," *High Times* 71, 1981, 36.
45 Robert Falconer, "He Is Legend," *CinemaSpy.com*, accessed December 11, 2007, http://www.cinemaspy.com/article.php?id=379.
46 Steve "Capone" Prokopy, "AICN Exclusive: Capone chews it with George Romero in first extended interview regarding Land of the Dead!" *Ain't It Cool News*, July 19, 2004, http://www.aintitcool.com/node/17989.
47 Ernest Becker, "A Note on Freud's Primal Horde Theory," *Psychoanalytic Quarterly* 30 (1961): 413.
48 Waller, *The Living and the Undead*, 278.
49 Daniel C. Dennett, *Consciousness Explained* (New York: Little, Brown and Co., 1991), 73.
50 Brent Adkins, *Death and Desire in Hegel, Heidegger, and Deleuze* (Edinburgh: Edinburgh University Press, 2007), 180–1.
51 Waller, *The Living and the Undead*, 280.
52 Ibid., 281.
53 Ibid., 283.
54 Ibid., 284, 286.
55 Ibid., 287.
56 Ibid.
57 Adkins, *Death and Desire in Hegel, Heidegger, and Deleuze*, 182.
58 Waller, *The Living and the Undead*, 314.
59 Hand, "Proliferating Horrors," 117.
60 Hand, "Proliferating Horrors," 128.
61 Ibid., 129–30.
62 Ibid., 129.
63 Falconer, "He Is Legend."
64 Hand, "Proliferating Horrors," 128.
65 See Dodd Alley, *Gamers and Gorehounds—The Influence of Video Games on the Contemporary American Horror Film* (Saarbrücken, Germany: Verlag Dr Müller Aktiengesellschaft & Co., 2007).
66 Hand, "Proliferating Horrors," 134.
67 Alain Silver and James Ursini, *The Zombie Film: From White Zombie to World War Z* (Milwaukee, WI: Applause Theatre & Cinema, 2014), 271.
68 Silver and Ursini, *The Zombie Film*, 274.
69 *Doc of the Dead*, directed by Alexandre O. Philippe (Denver, CO: Exhibit A Pictures, 2014), DVD.

70 See, for example, Neil McRobert, "Shoot Everything That Movies: Post-Millennial Zombie Cinema and the War on Terror," *Textus* 25, no. 3 (2012): 103–16; Nicole Birch-Bayley, "Terror in Horror Genres: The Global Media and the Millennial Zombie," *The Journal of Popular Culture* 45, no. 6 (2012): 1137–51; and Kyle Bishop, "Dead Man *Still* Walking: Explaining the Zombie Renaissance," *Journal of Popular Film and Television* 37, no. 1 (2009): 16–25.

71 Kyle Bishop, "Dead Man *Still* Walking: Explaining the Zombie Renaissance," *Journal of Popular Film and Television* 37, no. 1 (2009): 16–25.

72 Max Brooks, *The Zombie Survival Guide: Complete Protection from the Living Dead* (New York: Three Rivers Press, 2003).

73 I am grateful to WorldCat for helping me to locate and document the materials contained in this bibliography.

74 Žižek, *Organs Without Bodies*, 136.

2
Zombie Masses: Monsters for the Age of Global Capitalism
David R. Castillo

Abstract: *This chapter re-examines the current zombie craze in the context of a discussion of modern monsters. From abnormal births to witches and vampires to today's zombie masses, monsters have populated our imagination since the dawn of modernity. Going back to the late middle ages and the early modern period, monsters have been interpreted as both* signs *and* warnings, *in accordance with etymologies that traced the word "monster" to the Latin verbs* monstrare *(to show or reveal) and* monere *(to warn or admonish). Taking this notion as a point of departure, this chapter asks and seeks to answer the following questions: Why is it that our favorite monsters today are undead humans, i.e., vampires and, especially, zombies?*

Castillo, David R., David Schmid, David A. Reilly and John Edgar Browning. *Zombie Talk: Culture, History, Politics.* New York: Palgrave Macmillan, 2016. DOI: 10.1057/9781137567727.0006.

Monsters

The etymology of the term *monster* has been traced to the Latin word *monstrum* (from *mostrare*, meaning to show, reveal, expose, unveil, display). This connection between the monster and the act of revealing (*mostrare*, and even *demonstrare*) was firmly established by Saint Augustine and his followers. The term has also been linked to the Latin verb *monere* (to warn or admonish). This second ascription has gained ground more recently in etymological dictionaries, often associated with the description of abnormal births thought to prognosticate impending disasters.[1] Whether they are viewed as signs of the divine will or interpreted as providential warnings, monsters have been "read" as *bodies pregnant with meaning* for much of the history of Western culture.

In the ancient world, hybrid creatures were also thought of as monsters, although not always evil: the mandrake is a cross between a human and a plant, the centaur between a man and a horse, Pegasus between a horse and a bird, the siren between a woman and a bird, and so on. Yet, as the dualistic Judeo-Christian tradition became dominant in Western culture, hybridity, abnormality, and the crossing of boundaries were increasingly associated with transgression, moral deformity, and evil intent. Hence, the abnormality of the monster would come to be widely interpreted in European culture as defiance of law, be it the natural law or the established political and moral orders. The entry for *monstro* in Covarrubias's *Tesoro de la Lengua* (1611) reads in part "cualquier parto contra la regla y orden natural,"[2] ("any birth against the norm and order of nature"). Similarly, Covarrubias's French contemporary Jean Riolan discusses monstrosity in connection with the "perverted" nature of hermaphrodites in a 1614 essay. He argues that the sexual hybridity of hermaphrodite monsters is "a perversion of the order of natural causes, the health of the people, and the authority of the king."[3]

While monsters inspire fear, apprehension and revulsion in (early) modern times, they are also objects of fascination in the curiosity culture of the Renaissance and the baroque, and later in the Romantic period and beyond. In her insightful book *Una era de monstruos: Representaciones de lo deforme en el Siglo de Oro español*, Elena del Río Parra documents the existence of an early modern tradition within which monsters are viewed as fascinating rarities. Seventeenth-century author Rivilla Bonet y Pueyo, for example, remarks that monstrous births are worthy of curiosity and admiration for their novelty and rarity. His definition of *monstro* extends to encompass anything admirable due to an excess of malice, but also of goodness: "cualquier cosa admirable, no sólo por exceso de malicia, sino tambien de bondad."[4] The admirable excess of which this seventeenth-century author speaks may be linked to the pursuit of the "extreme" in baroque poetry, art and architecture.[5] More importantly for our purposes, this fascination with the rare nature of monsters and their excesses is at the root of the modern aesthetics of the fantastic.

As I have argued elsewhere,[6] the modern fantastic is born in the context of the culture of curiosities of the sixteenth and seventeenth centuries, at the meeting place between certainty and doubt, and between apprehension and fascination. We are very much curious about the monsters we fear. We may be utterly repulsed by them, but we are also fascinated by their extraordinary nature, their perverted views, and their deviant behavior. As Barbara Benedict writes apropos English wonder tales and foundational Gothic fictions from *A Wonder in Staffordshire* (1661), *The Hartfordshire Wonder* (1669), and *Admirable Curiosities of England* (1682) to Horace Walpole's *The Castle of Otranto* (1764) and William Beckford's *Vathek* (1782): "[W]onder tales and Gothic fictions...redefined curiosity as an aesthetic enterprise....Imaginary literature became the new arena for the exploration of forbidden areas and the testing of truth."[7]

In Spain, the literary exploration of forbidden areas inhabited by monsters can be traced back to the late Renaissance and early baroque miscellanea, especially to Antonio de Torquemada's *Jardín de flores curiosas* (1570) and Julián de Medrano's *La silva curiosa* (1583). These textual cabinets of curiosities incorporated sensationalist "news" and macabre stories and, in some cases, elaborate accounts of preternatural experiences that tested natural, moral, and epistemological boundaries. If other texts from the period, including teratology treatises and *relaciones de sucesos*, offer detailed descriptions of hybrid creatures, abnormal births, and other curiosities, the dark tales included in *Jardín de flores curiosas* and *La silva curiosa* draw a direct link between the figure of the monster and the mysterious realms of the preternatural and the occult.

Torquemada underscores the dreadful consequences of the witch's crossing of natural and moral boundaries. Even accidental exposure to the witch's craft results in monstrous forms of self-alienation in *Jardín de flores curiosas*. By contrast, the pursuit of forbidden knowledge, even black magic, is actually celebrated, rather than punished, in *La silva curiosa*. Thus, the dominant textual presence in Medrano's text is an eccentric first-person narrator, Julio, who is himself a sort of monster obsessed with morbid themes, forbidden knowledge, and perverse lifestyles. The two central characters of *La silva*'s final section, "Parte de los epitaphios curiosos hallados por Julio," are Christóbal Salvage, a sorcerer who collects morbid objects and evil spells, and Orcavella, an undead witch who feeds on the blood of innocent children. The narrator refers to both of these characters as *monstros de natura*.

Early modern ghost stories and dark fantasies involving evil monsters like Christóbal Salvage and Orcavella are in fact, as I argued in *Baroque Horrors*, the direct predecessors of the better known Gothic horrors. Clearly Salvage and Orcavella represent a different breed of monster than their Gothic counterparts (full blown literary horrors such as Vathek, Frankenstein, Mr. Hyde, Dorian Gray, and Dracula), but they all express and negotiate deep-seeded anxieties about the consequences of human trespasses of the natural, social, and moral orders. As Joseph Conrad perceptively observed in a 1917 letter, "[f]ashions in monsters do change, but the truth of humanity goes on for ever, unchangeable and inexhaustible in the variety of its disclosures."[8] Whether we are considering nineteenth-century or twenty-first-century horrors, or their late sixteenth-century predecessors, I would suggest that the revelations and warnings that come with our dark fantasies are both enduring and historically specific. Thus, death (to provide a particularly apt example) may well be a trans-historical source of anxiety, but our dark fantasies reflect/reshape our anxiety about death in historically specific modes. This is why, when it comes to taking stock of the meaning of horror fiction, I see social-historical and political readings, and feminist and psychoanalytic approaches as ultimately complementary, in so far as they help us understand different aspects of our favorite monsters and their dwelling places.[9]

Vampires

Sorcerers and witches are still popular in our literary and cinematic imagination, but they tend to show up in fairy tales and adventure-type fantasies such as the *Lord of the Rings* and *Harry Potter* sagas. Even vampires and werewolves have recently crossed over into coming-of-age teenage fantasies starting with the popular TV show *Buffy the Vampire Slayer*, and continuing with the hit series *The Vampire Diaries* and the *Twilight* book and movie phenomenon. In these, as well as in adult-oriented novels, movies, and TV series—such as Anne Rice's *The Vampire Chronicles* and their film adaptations, and the current TV series *True Blood* and *Dracula*—vampires and humans are sometimes difficult to distinguish from one another. Vampires are often "humanized" in these pop culture blockbusters. In the case of *True Blood*, the point is not necessarily that vampires are humanized, but, more accurately, that humanity is "vampirized"; that is, humans are represented as vampire-like monsters who are just as likely to prey on the vampires as the vampires are to prey on them.

True Blood goes further than *Buffy*, *The Vampire Diaries* and *Twilight* in projecting a fantasy world in which vampires and humans may coexist, thanks in part to the mass-production of a blood substitute for vampire consumption. The availability of this nutritional product allows some vampires to come out of the closet, so to speak. Their integration into mainstream society proves difficult, nonetheless, since most humans continue to think of them as evil spawns and dangerous predators. Many humans show scorn for those who associate with vampires. Their mantra is "God hates fangs." Similarly, most vampires disapprove of those from within their ranks who treat humans as equals rather than as an inferior race. The mistrust between humans and vampires is exacerbated by the persistence of vampires who live clandestine lives while refusing to give up their favorite meal: human blood. The most intriguing twist of the series, however, has to do with the fact that vampire blood is shown to have hallucinogenic and sense-enhancing properties if consumed by humans. This leads to the development of blood markets that exploit vampires as well as humans. Hence, the series features a number of elaborate and graphic scenes in which human predators capture and immobilize vampires in order to harvest their precious blood to either consume it themselves or to sell it in the drug market.

We can say that *True Blood* makes explicit what some critics see as an implicit or latent yet central element in the modern tradition of vampire fiction going back to Bram Stoker's *Dracula*. What I have in mind here is not simply *the return of the repressed*, at least not in the general sense in which werewolves and characters like Mr. Hyde represent a regression to a primal animality that lurks deep inside of us, hidden under layers of civilizing safeguards. Instead, I am thinking of the "economic repressed" that Karl Marx remarked upon when he referred to capital as a vampire-like machine, "a circulating thing which gains its energy only by preying upon 'living labor.'"

Prior to the nineteenth century, the figure of the vampire was mostly found in folk tales, which, as Ken Gelder[10] notes, grounded him into a localized spot. Thus, the vampire was essentially a local or regional monster. By contrast, more recent vampires are defined by extensive circulation through and across regional and national boundaries. In Bram Stoker's *Dracula*, the ancient vampire uproots himself from his native land of Transylvania, deep inside the Carpathian mountains, to travel to London, at the very center of the British empire, where he plans to "satiate his lust for blood and create a new and ever-widening circle of semi-demons to batten on the helpless." In its updated "world-traveler" version, the vampire may be seen as an apt mirror-image of the colonizer. Stephen Arata[11] has called attention to this intriguing aspect of Stoker's novel. As he argues in "The Occidental Tourist: *Dracula* and the Anxiety of Reverse Colonization":

> The novel thus sets up an equivalence between Harker and Dracula: one can be seen as an Orientalist travelling East, the Other—unsettling thought for Stoker's Victorian readers—as an Occidentalist travelling West.... Dracula's preoccupation with English culture is not motivated by a disinterested desire for knowledge; instead, his Occidentalism represents the essence of bad faith, since it both promotes and masks the Count's sinister plan to invade and exploit Britain and her people. By insisting on the connections between Dracula's growing knowledge and his power to exploit, Stoker also forces us to acknowledge how Western imperial practices are implicated in certain forms of knowledge. Stoker continually draws our attention to the affinities between Harker and Dracula, as in the oft-cited scene where Harker looks for Dracula's reflection in the mirror and sees only himself.[12]

If Stoker's *Dracula* can be read as a mirror-image of the colonizer, a personification of the "late-Victorian nightmare of reverse colonization,"[13] more recent novels have provided historically updated and nuanced versions of the "economic repressed" that may be revealed in and through the vampire metaphor. Thus, the iconic blood-sucking monster has presently been called upon to personify the institution of slavery in its modern version, and also to represent the predatory practices of global corporations in our post-colonial world. In his best-selling novel *Abraham Lincoln Vampire Hunter* (2010), Seth Grahame-Smith re-imagines the figure of the vampire in the context of a fictionalized reconstruction of Civil War America. In Grahame-Smith's historical fantasy, the genuine American vampires are white southern aristocrats who feed on helpless black slaves.

While Stoker's Occidentalist vampire may work as "a metaphor for capital"[14] in the colonial age, Grahame-Smith's Americanization of the vampire theme turns this old world monster into an allegory of modern slavery. The novel's graphic scenes of mechanized blood extraction are particularly telling in this regard. Here is a good example:

> Only now did I see the dark glass tubes running over our heads, running from the bodies on our left to the vessels on our right. Only now did I see the blood running into those vessels, kept warm by a row of tiny gas flames beneath. Only now did I see the chests of these "corpses" moving with each shallow breath. And here the whole horror of it struck me.[15]

The narrator's detailed description of the mechanized harvesting of blood from the bodies of immobilized slaves who are kept alive solely for this purpose suggests that this extreme form of human predation (the peculiar institution) ought not to be thought of as a "residual horror" or a left-over byproduct of a bygone era, but rather as a modern form of violence and exploitation. This may begin to explain why, despite its obvious cinematic plasticity, the above-quoted scene from Grahame-Smith's novel did not make it into the film adaptation, a mainstream shoot-them-up that was released with the same title as the book in 2012.

We can find similar scenes of mechanized blood extraction in the vampire trilogy co-authored recently by Guillermo del Toro and Chuck Hogan, especially in the third novel of the series *The Night Eternal* (2011). Here the "efficient extraction and packaging of human blood"[16] takes place in slaughter houses that have been converted into "blood factories"[17] following the Master's imperialist design. The Master is a Dracula-like figure whose American success is largely dependent on his business sense and his ability to understand the *mathematics of power* in corporate America: "The Master learned to align himself with influential power brokers.... He devised a formula for the mathematics of power. The perfect balance of vampires, cattle, and wardens."[18] I interpret these references to the Master's mathematics of power as a cautionary note directed against corporate America. Thus, in keeping with the logic behind Moreti's and Arata's "economic" readings of Stoker's classic work, I would argue that the novelistic trilogy co-authored by del Toro and Hogan accomplishes an insightful and effective updating of the vampire metaphor for our own post-colonial time. Briefly stated, the Master's vampire regime may be read as a dark metaphor of the objectifying tyranny of the present global market.

Zombies

As offspring of the romantic age of horrors, it is true enough that most modern vampires channel psychosexual anxieties; this is most evident today in the *Twilight* novels and movie phenomenon and popular TV series like *The Vampire Diaries*. These attractive vampires seem to have very little in common with the zombie version of the undead. On the other hand, and this is the point I am trying to make here, the tradition of vampire fantasies represented by *True Blood*, *The Strain*, and *Abraham Lincoln Vampire Hunter*, among other literary and film offerings of the last few years, coincide in foregrounding another equally significant dimension of the modern vampire, one that's intimately connected with the history of capitalism. This is the socio-symbolic zone where vampires and zombies meet as embodiments of the economic repressed, although I would argue that the zombie masses provide a more accurate picture, an image that's closer to the true face of the beast, precisely because there is nothing in it to hide or veil its ugly soul, as in the iconic picture of Dorian Gray.

It is important to remember that the zombie monsters were not always cannibalistic masses of walking corpses. Traditional African and Haitian zombies had no appetite for human flesh. In fact, they were often thought of as "slaves" either awakened from the dead or hypnotized into a magically induced catatonic state to carry out the will of the zombie master (or those who employed his services), as in the early film *White Zombie* (1932), directed and produced by brothers Victor and Edward Halperin (see Browning's chapter in this volume). In *White Zombie* we can see the division of (zombie) labor that best represents the masculine fantasies of colonial powers: masses of dark-skinned colonial subjects "recruited" for slave work, on the one hand, and a carefully sexualized female "white zombie" who is hypnotized into "romantic" submission, on the other. The theatrical poster makes it clear that this is in fact the point of a female "white zombie": "*With these zombie eyes, he rendered her powerless; with this zombie grip, he made her perform his every desire.*"

In the literary field, the first full-fledged zombie story of which I am aware also features a "white zombie," in this case a married lady who is forced into "adulterous" sexual services by means of black magic. The story is part of a dark collection of baroque novellas authored by proto-feminist writer María de Zayas, published in Spain in 1647 with the title *Desengaños amorosos* or *Disenchantments of Love*. The collection—which has often been deemed "obscene" and even "pornographic"—has recently been hailed by feminist critics as a hard-hitting denunciation of violence against women and a clever exposé of the dark aspects of the "architecture of patriarchy" in the aristocratic society of seventeenth-century Spain.[19]

Those who are familiar with *White Zombie* will recognize the key ingredients of Zayas's *Innocence Punished*: a powerful lord blinded by passion, an innocent lady who "belongs" to another man, and a carefully racialized zombie master (in this case a Moorish necromancer), who performs the necessary enslaving rituals. In Zayas's novella, the lady is turned into an actual sex slave who literally sleepwalks into her victimizer's bed in a trance-like state. Although the rapist is eventually exposed and prosecuted for his crimes, the innocent lady is further victimized by her own husband, brother and sister-in-law, all of whom conspire to imprison her inside a wall of the house as punishment for her involuntary adultery. It would be left to her rotting body to tell the story of her victimization when she is finally freed after six years of horrifying entombment:

> She was blind...; her lovely tresses, which when she entered were strands of gold, white as the very snow, tangled and full of little animals...her color, the color of death, so thin and emaciated that her bone showed as if the skin on top of them were but a thin veil...; her clothes turned to ashes so that most parts of her body were visible; her feel and legs bare, because the excrement from her body, since she had nowhere to dispose of it, had not only eaten into them, but her very flesh was eaten up to the thighs with wounds and worms, which filled the stinking place.[20]

Graphic representations of "death in life" are not out of place in the art and literature of the baroque period, yet this picture of decaying flesh is not offered as a reflection on the transitory nature of human existence, as in traditional baroque *vanitas* or *memento mori*, but as evidence of the silent victimization of women that takes place inside the walls of aristocratic houses in Imperial Spain. As I have argued elsewhere:

> The monsters come with the house in Zayas's baroque tales of kinship and terror. At the end [of her novella collection], we are left with nothing but dead bodies and ruins everywhere. This is an implosion of the aristocratic house not unlike Poe's vision of decay and destruction in "The Fall of the House of Usher."[21]

Hence, in terms of our own cultural horizon, the "politics" of Zayas's zombie story seem closer to the anti-establishment George A. Romero films of the 1960s and 1970s than to the early *White Zombie*, despite the thematic coincidences we have outlined between the 1647 novella written by Zayas and the 1932 film directed by the Halperin brothers.

Since the release of Romero's classic *Night of the Living Dead* (1968), the walking dead are imagined in cinematic fantasies and print fiction as agents of the apocalypse. In the literary field, we can trace the apocalyptic treatment of the undead to Richard Matheson's masses of zombie-vampires in the visionary novel *I Am Legend* (1954), which has been adroitly adopted for the big screen on several occasions (see Browning's chapter in this volume). Remarkably, in the post-Matheson and post-Romero zombie culture, the rise of the dead is most often envisioned as a cataclysmic byproduct of the progress of human technology. This is something that the new walking dead share with the monstrous machines featured in such blockbuster fantasies as *The Terminator* and *The Matrix* sagas. Like robots and computers, zombies have no soul. Yet while the rise of the machines is motivated by their will to power, the rise of the dead is aimless. Unlike vampires and rebellious machines, Romero's walking dead have no agenda and no will. They are driven by an insatiable and unexplained appetite for living human flesh.

To be sure, Romero's "classic" zombies have no *anima*, no internal life-principle. They are animated instead by an outside force. Their behavior is remarkably similar to Terminator-style automatons, machines programmed to kill; except that there is no programmer and no master design behind their (up)rising. Unlike the "domestic" zombies associated with West African and South African religions and Haitian folklore, Romero's herds of walking dead have nothing to do with mystical or spiritualist practices. They are simply cannibalistic masses of decaying human flesh.

In the last few years, zombie fantasies have flooded the horror and sci-fi markets. They have taken over much of our popular print culture, as well as our screens, with such best-selling novels as Max Brook's *World War Z* (2006) (now a major motion picture), short story collections like *The Living Dead*, comic book and TV series such as *The Walking Dead*, and countless video games. In fact, the walking dead have stepped outside the boundaries of fiction to show up in the streets of our most populous cities, even in own news cycles. Nowadays, it seems that every major town must host its own zombie walk. Remarkably, the CDC (The Centers for Disease Control and Prevention) has had to issue zombie related statements.

On June 4, 2012, I received an intriguing email request from columnist Fred Grimm of *The Miami Herald*. The message illustrates the extent to which the zombie craze has taken hold of the public's imagination:

For the last 10 days, Miami has been riveted by the story of a nude, apparently psychotic man, perhaps under the influence of some drug, who attacked and nearly killed a homeless man, ripping off most of the fellow's face with his teeth before a policeman shot and killed the assailant. Since, all sort of references have bubbled up about, among other things, a Zombie virus. As mindless as this premise might be, apparently the Centers for Disease Control in Atlanta felt compelled to issue a statement: "The flesh-eating living dead don't actually exist," said a spokesman for the Centers for Disease Control and Prevention (CDC). "CDC does not know of a virus or condition that would reanimate the dead (or one that would present zombie-like symptoms)," agency spokesman David Daigle told the Huffington Post. I had already been thinking about the peculiar prevalence of Zombies and Vampires and Werewolves in our pop culture, with probably more references in TV and movies and books than religion. I just wonder...if folks like you have some explanation for this quirk in contemporary culture.

The Miami Herald would subsequently publish Grimm's article on the subject on June 5, 2012 with the title "Fear, anxiety drive zombie craze." While my own response arrived a few hours too late and therefore did not make it into the published piece, Grimm's article incorporated comments from Southern Utah University English professor Kyle Bishop and SUNY-Buffalo English professor David Schmid (a co-author of this volume), as well as from University of South Florida anthropology professor Elizabeth Bird. Notably, they all coincide in pointing out that our present fascination with monsters, especially zombies, bespeaks of—in Schmid's words—"a society riven by fears and anxieties of various kinds, including uncertainty about the future."[22] In the same article, Kyle Bishop, author of *American Zombie Gothic* (2010), is quoted as saying, "I thought we as a culture were simply seeing a renewed and increased interest in monster narratives as a gut-check reaction to 9/11 and the War on Terror. Now, however, the zombie has become something much more visceral, something that has taken hold of our collective unconscious."[23] For her part, Bird notes that we use "our monsters to try to explain our society (and vice versa)," which is why zombies have become our favorite surrogates when it comes to expressing the fear of nuclear and pandemic catastrophes and environmental collapse, as well as "the idea that we are consuming ourselves."[24]

If the modern vampire may have functioned as an apt metaphor for the predatory practices of capital in colonial and post-colonial societies, the zombie hordes may best express present anxieties about the dreadful

50   David R. Castillo

[margin note: zombies speak about consumerism]
[margin note: perils of capitalism?]

fate of a world inhabited by post-human crowds of <u>mindless, soulless consumers</u>.²⁵ I would further argue that our fixation with apocalyptic fantasies—world-wide zombie plagues, nuclear disasters, environmental collapse, and other man-made catastrophes—is fundamentally tied to the widespread conviction that there is no possible alternative to capitalism as a world-wide economic system, paired with the growing realization, or at least the suspicion, that the logical evolution of <u>global capitalism will inexorably lead to our self-destruction</u>.²⁶ In a famous scene of Romero's second zombie film, *Dawn of the Dead* (1978), a group of zombies approaches the shopping mall where the survivors have taken refuge. One of the survivors looks out beyond the glass doors and says "They are us." Could this be the fundamental revelation of Romero's films? Are we the true zombies? Masses of walking dead driven by insatiable, senseless, catastrophic consumption? This revelation would indeed come with a grim warning about our present and immediate future: the end of the human race (an apocalypse of our own making) is upon us!

When we examine the latest products of the global zombie culture, it appears as though the zombie masses that have taken away—literally swallowed up—our future are intent in cannibalizing the past as well. A perfect example of this recent twist in zombie literature is Seth Grahame-Smith's *Pride and Prejudice and Zombies* (2009), a seemingly parodic reworking of Jane Austin's nineteenth-century classic. The book cover emphasizes this parodic distance: "An expanded edition of the beloved Jane Austin novel featuring all new scenes of bone-crunching zombie mayhem.... Complete with romance, heartbreak, swordfights, cannibalism, and thousands of rotting corpses, *Pride and Prejudice and Zombies* transforms a masterpiece of world literature into something you'd actually want to read."²⁷ Yet, in reading this bastardized version of Austin's novel, I couldn't shake the impression that much of Grahame-Smith's "expanded edition" functions as a pastiche, rather than a parody, in that it merely accentuates the ironic tone of Austin's original work and her sharp criticism of the idle British aristocracy of the early nineteenth century. Thus, the presence of zombies seems to underscore the monstrous (cannibal) nature of a decadent aristocratic body that feeds on the life-energy of local workers and distant colonial subjects.

This characterization could easily apply to the fourth installment in the Romero zombie franchise, *Land of the Dead*. Arguably, the most interesting characteristic of this 2005 film is a trope experimented with in Romero's *Day of the Dead* (1985): the *learning zombie*. As one of the human survivors in *Land of the Dead* put it at the very beginning of the film, "they are trying to be us...learning to be us...it's like they are pretending to be alive." By the end of the movie, the zombies seem to have re-acquired some primitive communication skills, a surprising degree of self-consciousness, even a sense of kinship, and a growing recognition of their true enemy, not the dispossessed human masses, but the opulent elite who have barricaded themselves inside high-end apartments in the middle of a luxury shopping high rise. Their exclusive (membership only) community of CEOs and shoppers is surrounded by concentric circles of exploited humanity. If there is a ray of hope in Romero's post-apocalyptic vision, this is quite simply the hope of a successful revolution of the (undead) masses.

Today, the blockbuster TV show *The Walking Dead* follows in the footsteps of Romero's classic zombie films. The show and the graphic novels that inspire it are constructed around the same ingredients: an apocalyptic pandemic that turns humans into walking corpses inexplicably hungry for human flesh, and—even more importantly—a focus on the group dynamics of the survivors. As in *Land of the Dead*, all of humanity has been infected with the zombie virus, which means that everyone is a latent "walker" who will inevitably reawake as a zombie cannibal regardless of how they die. More than any other product of the current zombie culture, *The Walking Dead* spotlights decision-making as the endangered trait (and obligation) that defines our humanity. Decoupled from the comforts of daily routines and the familiar, consumer-oriented notion of "choice"—i.e., choosing between products available for purchase—the act of decision-making takes on a renewed urgency and a transcendent charge as a matter of ineludible individual and collective responsibility, often accompanied by a close examination of mainstream moral values and political principles.

One has to wonder whether the spectators of *Land of the Dead* and *The Walking Dead* might not get more than they bargained for when their moral principles and beliefs and their political structures are crudely dissected, and in some cases exposed as little more than hypocritical, or even cynical, compromises resulting from their blind acceptance of an exploitative status quo and their willful denial of inconvenient truths. But of course, this is part of the attraction of post-apocalyptic novels, films, and TV shows such as the NBC series *Revolution*, as well as "teen" literary and movie phenomena like *The Hunger Games* and *Divergent*. The author of *Divergent*, Veronica Roth, commented on this fundamental aspect of post-apocalyptic fantasies in an interview included as "bonus materials" in the first novel of her best-selling trilogy. The question posed to her is, "Why do you feel people are naturally drawn to reading books about dystopian societies?" Her response may be helpful here: "Dystopian books are perfect for people who like to ask 'what if?'.... The majority of the characters in dystopian and post-apocalyptic literature have a lot of agency—they take charge of their lives in environments that make it hard for them to do so."[28]

Post-apocalyptic narratives offer their audiences the fantasy of a *zero point from which we can all* (vicariously at least) start over. We get to step out of our routines, our comforts, our safeguards; we get to reimagine ourselves dealing with the hardships, the dangers, the responsibilities, the demands, and the raw relationships that come with the post-apocalyptic landscape. We get to ask not only "What if?"—as Roth says—but "Who would we be(come)? What kind of decisions would we make? How would we organize our thoughts and emotions? How would we relate to others and negotiate our identities? What kind of behavioral patterns would we establish as individuals and communities? How would we reimagine our civic and political structures?"

Symptomatically perhaps, in the latest wave of post-apocalyptic narratives, certainly in the products of the current zombie culture, the "rebirth" of the individual is directly associated with acts of extreme violence: shooting, stubbing, crashing, burning (in)human bodies. A sinister version of the Cartesian ego seems to rule the post-apocalyptic landscape: I kill, therefore I am (*Cogito ergo* [*caedō*])! Though, to be fair, some of these same movies, novels, and TV shows entertain "pacifist" alternatives as well. In *The Hunger Games*, the final refusal of Katniss and Peeta to obey the mandate to kill (in this case, kill or attempt to kill each other) is offered at the conclusion of the first novel of the series as an act of defiance of violent powers, an affirmation of their shared humanity, and a sign of communal hope.

At times, *The Walking Dead* seems to move in this same direction when our reluctant heroes hesitate, or even refuse to pull the trigger, as when Rick trades the gun for the rake in his determination to become a farmer. But these moments of "dis-investment" in the violent destiny of the post-apocalyptic world are "by necessity" short-lived in zombie-plagued landscapes. Productive, nurturing, and non-violent life-styles are simply unsustainable, even explicitly suicidal, in these

[Handwritten annotation at top: "zombie movies align w/ pro gun culture?"]

relentlessly dangerous environments. This permanent survival mode, which requires constant acts of violence, is the reason why zombie fantasies appear to align so closely with pro-gun culture, as Browning argues in this volume, and possibly with libertarian and/or pro-militia movements and ideology and vigilante justice. In the end, the difference between our favorite post-apocalyptic heroes (say Rick in *The Walking Dead*) and their human arch-enemies (the Governor, for example) has to do with their measured administering of violence, not so much against the masses of walking dead (this is, for the most part, a given, with the notorious exception of Romero's *Land of the Dead*), but against other living humans. They must be capable of selective, surgical, and judicious (yet extreme and murderous) destruction. In this sense, the tragic heroes of *The Walking Dead* have something in common with their counterparts in traditional Hollywood epics, from the drifters that populate the Western genre, to the Stallone, Segal, and Vin Diesel vigilante-types of more recent blockbusters.

Zombies Exported

The Romero-style zombie monsters are by all accounts thriving in the present global market. Zombie movies, TV shows, novels, and games are among the most successful "exports" of the current culture industry. In Spain, we can find scores of walking dead fantasies, most of which have been published in recent years, including your run-of-the-mill zombie apocalypse, as well as more nuanced parodies and pastiches. In January 2006 a young Spanish lawyer, Manel Loureiro posted a blog with the title *Apocalipsis Z*. As the number of daily visitors reached the half million mark, Loureiro secured a contract with Dolmen to publish a print version of the blog. The printed text came out in 2007 with the same title. Since, Dolmen has published dozens of Spanish language zombie fantasies in its dedicated series Línea Z, including Carlos Sisí's *Los Caminantes*, which went through fifteen reprints between 2009 and 2012, and its equally popular sequel *Necrópolis*. Loureiro ended up publishing the continuation of *Apocalipsis Z* in two volumes that came out in the well-established press Plaza Janés, *Los días oscuros* (2010) and *La ira de los justos* (2011). For his part, Carlos Sisí would also venture outside of Dolmen's Línea Z with the third volume of his zombie trilogy, *Los Caminantes: Hades Nebula*, published by Minotauro in 2011.

DOI: 10.1057/9781137567727.0006

What attracts consumers to zombie gore?

The popularity of Loureiro's and Sisí's respective trilogies has significantly contributed to the current boom of zombie fiction in Spain. This boom includes many original Spanish language works, as well as a multitude of translations of English language zombie novels, short stories, zombie survival manuals, graphic novels, and so on. Most of these works do little but recreate the zombie apocalypse, Romero style, while piling on the gore. Among them, I have selected a few narratives for commentary based on my own sense of what constitutes novel or revealing trends and variations in zombie themes.

One of the most self-consciously spectacular offerings of the zombie subgenre in Spain is Víctor Conde's *Naturaleza muerta* (2009). As the title suggests, Conde arranges his graphic scenes of zombie gore as macabre still lifes. The book cover designed by Alejandro Colucci underscores this postmodern (or neobaroque) interdiscursive connection. Thus, Colucci's elaborate illustration is explicitly evocative of the traditional still life and *vanitas*. We can see a fruit basket filled with fresh apples and grapes, a wheel of cheese made to look like an old-fashioned clock, and several ceramic containers, resting on a clothed kitchen table, alongside objects that symbolize human knowledge, such as an old book and a quill. The picture is complete with a severed forearm resting near a few pieces of bread at the edge of a napkin, which partially covers fresh blood stains. In the background, a drawn curtain reveals a painted human skull at the bottom corner of what appears to be a baroque *vanitas*. Colucci's illustration effectively captures Conde's pictorial imagination and neobaroque gusto. The following passage is a good example of Conde's pictorial technique:

> Zurek permaneció fiel a su estoicismo incluso cuando vio como le arrancaban un cuarto de kilo de carne de sus michelines. Alargó desesperadamente las manos hacia atrás, intentando buscar un asidero para los dedos, pero lo que encontró fue un antebrazo amputado. Estaba tirado encima de una bandeja con vasos y jarras de cerámica. Al lado había un caballete caído sobre un macizo de gardenias. Captó la ironía del mensaje: alguien se había entretenido pintando una naturaleza muerta, mientras su pareja o sus hijos se bañaban en la piscina, sin llegar a sospechar que semejante elemento macabro quedaría añadido alguna vez al cuadro. En el fondo no alteraba el contenido, pues sólo había cosas muertas en la composición.[29]
>
> (Zurek remained loyal to his stoicism even as he saw how they severed a quarter of a kilogram of flesh from his midsection flab. He desperately stretched his hands backwards, in an attempt to find something his fingers

could hold, but what he found was an amputated forearm. It was lying on a tray with glasses and ceramic jars. Beside it, there was an easel fallen on a bed of gardenias. He realized the irony of the message: someone had been leisurely painting a still life, while his partner or kids were swimming in the pool, unsuspecting of the fact that such macabre element would add to the painting. In truth it didn't alter its meaning, since there were only dead things in the composition.)

Starting with the flesh severed from Zurek's midsection, and continuing with the amputated forearm of the anonymous artist displayed on a serving tray, alongside some glasses and ceramic containers, this scene may be best described as a macabre mis-en-abyme of "dead things." As the angle expands to include the immediate surroundings, we can see the artist's easel laying on a bed of gardenias, a final vision of destruction, but also the first image of something whole and alive in nature, not *naturaleza muerta*, but *naturaleza viva*. This final element of the composition allows us to draw a close connection with the novel's ending, which offers the same severe contrast, the same chiaro-oscuro, between "dead things" (the self-inflicted destruction of humanity) and the rapidly growing bed of invading greenery, which is said to be taking over the post-human Earth. Captain Piotr's view from his satellite post in outer space offers the ultimate opening of the lens: "bosque tipo pangea...verdor agresivo...naturaleza que se veía por fin libre de ese cáncer llamado Hombre...Naturaleza Viva"[30] ("Pangaea-type forest...aggressive greenery...nature that was finally free from the cancer of Man...Nature Alive.")

In this sense, Conde's *Naturaleza muerta* is not just a fictional chronicle of the death of humankind, but also a post-apocalyptic utopia of the rebirth of Nature. Ironically, both the zombie pandemia and the rebirth of nature are caused by exposure to the same radiation. The final destruction of the human race and the post-apocalyptic image of a resurging human-less planet Earth represent the fulfillment of the unauthorized translation of an Old Testament prophesy mentioned in an earlier passage: "una de las arcaicas traducciones del Antiguo Testamento...contenía un último capítulo en que se vaticinaba el fin de la humanidad y el reino de las bestias y de los árboles, y de todo lo natural que no incluyera a los hijos de Adán."[31] (One of the ancient translations of the Old Testament...contained a final chapter that prophesied the end of humanity and the kingdom of the beasts and the trees, and of the entire natural world, excluding the sons and daughters of Adam.)

DOI: 10.1057/9781137567727.0006

There are other moments in which the narrative reaches back into the past in search of ancient Judeo-Christian motifs and symbology that might offer grounds for speculation regarding the possibility of previous zombie (up)risings. Would the zombies have been present in the epoch-changing events of our past? Could they have been the key agents of history?

> Zurek se preguntó si el regreso de los muertos no se habría producido ya en varias ocasiones, a lo largo de la historia, y por lo tanto no era un suceso aislado y excepcional.... ¿Podrían haberse levantado los inquilinos de las fosas comunes de Europa y América para extender las plagas? ¿Se habría asentado tanto el cristianismo por la Europa aún humeante de las cenizas del Imperio Romano...gracias a que los testigos de aquellas plagas de pellejos vieron en ellas una prueba de que, efectivamente, existía la Resurrección? ¿Fue Jesús el primer zombie...y por eso regresó al tercer día para contaminar a los miembros que quedaban de su secta?[32]

> (Zurek wondered if the return of the dead would not have taken place on several occasions already, throughout history, and therefore it wasn't an isolated or exceptional event.... Would the dwellers of mass graves in Europe and America have turned up to extend the plagues? Would Christianity have advanced so quickly over the smoking ashes of the Roman Empire...thanks to the witnesses of zombie plagues who saw in them proof of the Resurrection? Was Jesus the first zombie...and that's why he returned on the third day to contaminate the remaining members of his sect?)

The notion that the undead may have walked the Earth in other historical periods is explored in a good number of recent novels, including *La muerte negra: El triunfo de los no-muertos* and *Quijote Z*, both authored by Házael G. González and published in 2010 in the Línea Z series of Dolmen. The first re-imagines the great plague of 1348 known as the Black Death as a zombie outbreak. The second plays on classic Cervantine motifs and situations, and on Cervantes's self-consciously parodic narrative style, to offer a bizarre pastiche featuring a man obsessed with zombie stories who takes to the road in order to become a zombie slayer.

Among the Spanish Golden Age classics, the anonymous *Lazarillo de Tormes* has been subjected to the same kind of zombie refurbishing in an Ediciones Debolsillo best-seller published with the title *Lazarillo Z: Matar zombis nunca fue pan comido*, signed by a Lázaro González-Pérez de Tormes. In this 2010 reworking of the original picaresque novel, first published in 1554, Lázaro becomes a heroic vampire warrior who fights a zombie plague that originated in the New World as a form of Indian revenge.³³ His fighting comrades are the "desechos de la Corona,"³⁴ a bizarre group of pícaros, prostitutes, and vampires, led by a homosexual nobleman and his morisco partner. In these macabre pastiches, the monstrous subject-matter spills over into its container. These are not just monster narratives, but *monstrous narratives*, zombie monstrosities in their own right. A perfect example of this type of self-conscious monstrosity is Hernán Migoya's zombie reconstruction of the recent political history of Spain in *Una, grande y zombie* (2011). Migoya's scandalous text features an undead Francisco Franco, who along with his sidekick Manuel Fraga, and a zombie army of politicians and journalists, led by the recently "converted" José Luis Rodríguez Zapatero and Mariano Rajoy, plan to resurrect the true and essential Spain: One, Great and Zombie. King Juan Carlos will also be "converted" to the imperial zombie cause near the end of the novel. In the final scene, the king and uncle Franco ("el tío Paco") will team up to devour his majesty's mistress whose ripped body, ready for consumption ("hecha lonchas"), appears to be offered as an allegory of the people of Spain: the Spain of flesh and blood.

Migoya's exhibitionist cynicism is reminiscent of the dark eccentricity of Medrano's early baroque fantasy in *La silva curiosa*, while his theatrical self-reflectivity seems closer to the Cervantine style, especially in those passages in which fiction and reality meet face to face, often spilling into each other. The discussion of the conventions of the zombie genre or subgenre in chapter 11, aptly titled, "Ateniéndose a los desechos," echoes similar conversations in *Don Quixote* regarding the conventions of chivalric and pastoral literature:

> El concepto de zombi también ha cambiado con la evolución de la cultura popular—apuntaló Pere.... Los zombis de ahora no son como los de hace cien años.... No fue hasta los años sesenta cuando George A. (la A es importante) Romero lo cambió todo con *La noche de los muertos vivientes*.... Él creó esa noción pesadillesca de una invasión de zombis global. Los muertos vivientes de hoy son realmente eso.³⁵

> (The concept of the zombie has also changed with the evolution of popular culture—noted Pere.... Today's zombies are not like those of a hundred years ago.... It wasn't until the sixties that George A. (the A is important) Romero changed everything with *The Night of the Living Dead*.... He created the nightmarish notion of a global zombie invasion. The living dead of today are really that.)

DOI: 10.1057/9781137567727.0006

The conversation between Pere and Evaristo, "el héroe de la película"[36] (the movie's hero), moves into the scatological terrain when Pere points out some inconsistencies in the standard treatment of the zombie material: "Todo el mundo sabe que los zombis no cagan, otra incoherencia del mito. Porque entonces, ¿adónde van a parar todos esos cuerpos humanos que se comen?"[37] ("Everyone knows that the zombies don't shit, another incoherence of the myth. So then, where do all those human bodies that they eat go?") Note the connection with the often cited conversation of don Quixote and Sancho about whether or not the bewitched defecate in *Don Quixote* II, 23.[38]

One of the more interesting "Cervantine" occurrences takes place in chapter 17, titled, "La corta marcha," when the participants in the "III Zombie Walk de Barcelona" come face to face with the real thing. The crowd is carrying movies, books, comics, posters, and other zombie paraphernalia, "variada zarandaja relativa al *merchandising* y oferta de ocio referida al fenómeno"[39] ("all that non-sensical stuff that goes with the *merchandising* and the marketing of the [zombie] phenomenon.") Some of the participants possess (and treasure) copies of Migoya's own book: "este libro que usted tiene abierto en sus manos."[40] The Cervantine trick of dragging his work into the fictional world of the text allows Migoya to tie his own zombie novel (and its publisher and readers) to the marketing ploys that he is exposing. When the participants of the zombie "simulacro"[41] finally meet the real zombies, they are first elated to come across such realistic hordes of parading comrades before they are literally swallowed up by the zombie phenomenon.

Speaking of being swallowed up by the zombie phenomenon, author Manuel Martín made a telling confession in the biographical note of his zombie novel *Noche de difuntos del 38* (2012). His candidly cynical disclosure is reminiscent of the pícaro's confession in the prologue of *Lazarillo de Tormes*, except that the confession of the anonymous sixteenth-century author was about the scandal of his life (*el caso*), while Martín's is about the scandal of his writing: "Además, sus señorías, el acusado declara, que con premeditada alevosía mutó una historia de terror ambientada en la batalla del Ebro para transformarla en una novela zombi, harto como estaba de recibir negativas a sus intentos de publicación"[42] ("Moreover, your lordships, the accused declares that he transformed, with premeditated treachery, a story of terror set in the midst of the battle of the Ebro into a zombie novel, for he was tired of receiving negative reactions in response to his attempts to publish his work.") Martín's confession is also an act of self-defense and an implicit accusation directed against the current culture industry (a zombie phenomenon in its own right), and against the (zombie) readers, i.e., those avid consumers of standardized zombie products that might have showed up for Migoya's "III Zombie Walk de Barcelona."

Jorge Fernández Gonzalo concluded in his monographic study *Filosofía zombi* (2011) that "the zombie represents at this point the myth of the postmodern man" (my translation).[43] With this assertion in mind, I would argue that Migoya's "Cervantine" treatment of the zombie phenomenon and Martín's Lázaro-style confession are helpful reminders of the true face of the (not so mythical) monster. On the one hand, the countless zombie books, movies, TV shows, and video games represent the kind of repetition of standardized models that we associate with marketing ploys and the dehumanizing objectification of mass culture. On the other, many of these same cultural products explicitly warn us about the devastating effects of the market forces that result in mindless and catastrophic mass-production and mass-consumption.

This self-reflective cynicism is why the zombie hordes are the perfect monsters for the age of global capitalism. *The zombie masses are us* in more ways than one: they are the face of globalization, our dark mirror image, our sweat shops, our landfills, our pollution, an infinitely reproducible and exportable product of the mass-culture industry, a sign of the times, and a warning of things to come. Robert Kirkman's tongue-in-cheek explanation of the success of his trademark zombie products, especially the TV version of *The Walking Dead*, exemplifies the cynical dimension of much of the current zombie culture. His comments, recorded in a *Rolling Stone* piece contributed by David Peisner, are both insightful and profoundly unsettling: "Apocalyptic storytelling is appealing when people are having apocalyptic thoughts. With the global economic problems and everything else, a lot of people feel we're heading into dark times. As bad as it is for society [laughs], I am benefiting greatly."[44]

Notes

I would like to thank *HIOL* for permission to publish this expanded version of my previous essay. Thanks also to my colleague and partner-in-crime Kari Winter, for her perceptive and insightful comments on earlier drafts.

1 Marie-Hélene Huet, "Introduction to *Monstrous Imagination*," in *The Horror Reader*, ed. Ken Gelder (New York: Routledge, 2000), 87.

2. Elena Del Río Parra, *Una era de monstruos: Representaciones de lo deforme en el Siglo de Oro español* (Madrid: Iberoamericana, 2003), 24.
3. Lorraine Daston and Katherine Park, *Wonders and the Order of Nature, 1150–1750* (New York: Zone Books, 1998), 203.
4. Del Río Parra, *Una era de monstruos*, 24.
5. See José Antonio Maravall, *La cultura del barroco: Análisis de una estructura histórica* (Barcelona: Ariel, 1975).
6. See David R. Castillo, *Baroque Horrors: Roots of the Fantastic in the Age of Curiosities* (Ann Arbor, MI: The University of Michigan Press, 2010).
7. Barbara Benedict, *A Cultural History of Early Modern Inquiry* (Chicago: University of Chicago Press, 2001), 180.
8. Joseph Conrad, "Turgenev," in *Notes on Life and Letters* (Garden City, NY: Double, Page & Company, 1921), 46.
9. For psychoanalytic and feminist approaches, see Julia Kristeva, *Powers of Horror: An Essay on Abjection*, trans. León Roudiez (New York: Columbia University Press, 1982), and Barbara Creed, *The Monstrous-Feminine: Film, Feminism, Psychoanalysis* (New York: Routledge, 1993). José Monleón's *A Specter Is Haunting Europe: A Sociohistorical Approach to the Fantastic* (Princeton: Princeton University Press, 1990) is a classic example of the social-historical treatment of the modern fantastic.
10. Ken Gelder, "Introduction to Part 5," in *The Horror Reader*, ed. Ken Gelder (New York: Routledge, 2000), 146.
11. Stephen Arata, "The Occidental Tourist: Dracula and the Anxiety of Reverse Colonization," in *The Horror Reader*, ed. Ken Gelder (New York: Routledge, 2000), 166.
12. Ibid., 170. Arata provides further evidence of this suggested equivalence between Harker and Dracula in the following passage:

    The text's insistence that these characters are capable of substituting for one another becomes most pressing when Dracula twice dons Harker's clothes to leave the Castle. Since on both occasions the Count's mission is to plunder the town, we are encouraged to see a correspondence between the vampire's actions and those of the travelling Westerner. The equivalence between these two sets of actions is underlined by the reaction of the town's people, who have no trouble believing that it really is Harker, the visiting Englishman, who is stealing their goods, their money, their children. The peasant woman's anguished cry—"Monster, give me my child!" (ibid., 60)—is directed at him, not Dracula.

13. Ibid., 166.
14. Franco Moretti, "Dialectic of Fear (Extract)," in *The Horror Reader*, ed. Ken Gelder (New York: Routledge, 2000), 149.
15. Seth Grahame-Smith, *Abraham Lincoln Vampire Hunter* (New York: Grand Central Publishing, 2010), 192.

16 Guillermo del Toro and Chuck Hogan, *The Night Eternal* (New York: HaperCollins Publishing, 2011), 206–7.
17 Ibid., 86.
18 Ibid., 213.
19 Margaret Greer, *Maria de Zayas Tells Baroque Tales of Love and the Cruelty of Men (Studies in Romance Literatures)* (University Park, PA: Pennsylvania State University Press, 2000) and Amy Williamsen, "Challenging the Code: Honor in María de Zayas," in *María de Zayas: The Dynamics of Discourse*, eds. Amy Williamsen and Judith Whitenack (Madison: Fairleigh Dickinson University Press, 1995), 170–91.
20 María de Zayas, *Desengaños amorosos*, Ed. Alicia Yllera (Madrid, Cátedra, 1983), 287.
21 Castillo, *Baroque Horrors*, 118.
22 Fred Grimm, "Fear, Anxiety Drive Zombie Craze," *The Miami Herald*, June 5, 2012, http://www.miamiherald.com/news/special-reports/causeway-attack/article1940366.html.
23 Ibid.
24 Ibid.
25 While the notion of the post-human can be traced back to different (and often conflicting) theorizations, such as those of Robert Pepperell (*The Posthuman Condition: Consciousness Beyond the Brain* [2003]) and Katherine Hayles (*How We Became Posthuman: Virtual Bodies in Cybernetics, Literature and Informatics* [1999]), this concept has been recently associated with the zombie phenomenon. See, for example, Deborah Christie and Sarah Juliet Lauro, eds., *Better Off Dead: The Evolution of the Zombie as Post-Human* (Bronx, NY: Fordham University Press, 2011).
26 As Slavoj Žižek writes in *The Ticklish Subject: The Absent Centre of Political Ontology* (London: Verso, 1999): "The horizon of social imagination no longer allows us to entertain the idea of an eventual demise of capitalism... everybody tacitly accepts that capitalism is here to stay" (218).
27 See Seth Grahame-Smith, *Pride and Prejudice and Zombies* (Philadelphia, PA: Quirk Productions, 2009).
28 Veronica Roth, "Bonus Materials," in *Divergent* (New York: Katherine Tegen Books, 2011), 5.
29 Víctor Conde, *Naturaleza muerta* (Palma de Mallorca: Dolmen, 2009), 296.
30 Ibid., 311.
31 Ibid., 241.
32 Ibid., 222.
33 Lázaro González Pérez de Tormes, *Lazarillo Z: Matar Zombies nunca fue pan comido* (Barcelona: Debolsillo, 2010), 167.
34 Ibid., 83.
35 Hernán Migoya, *Una, grande y zombie* (Barcelona: Ediciones B, 2011), 192.

36 Ibid., 192.
37 Ibid., 195.
38 See my discussion in Chapter 4 of *(A)Wry Views: Anamorphosis, Cervantes and the Early Picaresque* (West Lafayette, IN: Purdue University Press, 2001).
39 Ibid., 307.
40 Ibid.
41 Ibid., 308.
42 See the biographical note in Manuel Martín, *Noche de difuntos del 38* (Palma de Mallorca: Dolmen, 2012).
43 Jorge Fernández Gonzalo, *Filosofía zombi* (Barcelona: Editorial Anagrama, 2011), 195.
44 David Peisner, "Blood, Sweat, & Zombies," *Rolling Stone*, no. 1194, October 24, 2013, 55.

3
The Coming Apocalypses of Zombies and Globalization

David A. Reilly

Abstract: *The zombie genre has exploded into pop culture. But what is the attraction? What do zombies represent and why have they captured our interest? This chapter explores some of the answers and offers a novel hypothesis: in both the zombie apocalypse and the destructive path of globalization, individuals are empowered as states fail. Globalization has been described as a "Coming Anarchy" of fragmentation and homogenization that creates a sense of despair and powerlessness not unlike the onslaught of zombie hordes. Despite this, through an analysis of the diffusion process of zombification, this chapter argues that the common theme in both globalization and zombification is that the individual is empowered as the state collapses.*

Castillo, David R., David Schmid, David A. Reilly and John Edgar Browning. *Zombie Talk: Culture, History, Politics*. New York: Palgrave Macmillan, 2016. DOI: 10.1057/9781137567727.0007.

Introduction

They keep coming. In ever greater numbers they are right outside our door. They multiply. They adapt.

In pop culture they have become ubiquitous. They appear in locations and at times unexpectedly. Their infection seems to cross species: first human, then canines and felines, now garden gnomes.[1] We can't get enough of the stories, the opportunities to watch their slow and steady expansion. The contagion hypnotizes us and makes us want more. We seek out new ways to kill them, new ways to protect ourselves against them, new ways to assimilate them. And as much as we enjoy the struggle and the bloodshed, we seem to really enjoy having them around. And we are more than willing to pay for it.

The zombie industry has exploded. In 2011 *The Week* magazine estimated the economic impact at more than $5,000,000,000, and that was before *World War Z* topped the box office for 2013 at $202 million.[2] And the second largest grossing zombie movie of all time is 2012's *Hotel Transylvania*. *Plants vs. Zombies 2* was the most downloaded game in the iOS App Store for an extended period in 2013. The *Resident Evil* video games—which center on zombie outbreaks resulting from a virus released through biological weapons—have sold more than 60 million copies, and recently broke the record for the fastest-selling US/European digital title in video game corporation Capcom's history.[3] *Pride and Prejudice and Zombies* has been on the New York Times bestseller list along with *World War Z* and *The Zombie Survival Guide*.

Interest is growing; the growth of the zombie entertainment industry is steady and steep. This is also reflected in zombie products. Of course you can purchase t-shirts, decorations, brain-shaped gelatin molds, posters, action figures, and novelties. But are you concerned about the impending apocalypse? Then you can buy a cache of weapons specifically designed to repel zombies.[4] Or is it survival manuals and training that you want? That, too, can be arranged.[5] At Zombie Survival Army/Navy Supplies of Orlando,[6] you can even get street sweeping equipment for the post-apocalyptic clean-up.

Much of the impetus for this survivalist preparation is tongue-in-cheek fantasy play. However, the possibility of an apocalyptic event has a basis in scientific reality. Cracked.com has listed five of the most likely reasons that a zombie apocalypse will occur: brain parasites; neurotoxins; the real "rage virus," a human form of mad cow disease known as Creutzfeldt-Jakob virus; neurogenesis and the regeneration of dead cells—including brains; and nanotechnology that may be used for neuro-manipulation.[7] The recent Discovery Channel documentary *Zombie Apocalypse* begins with the observation, "Zombies are real.... They're just not what you think they are." It observes that "scientists have started to believe the unbelievable" and interviews "experts" such as Dr. Steven Schlozman of Harvard Medical School's Department of Psychiatry, who posits that a zombie outbreak could result from a mutated contagion, most likely a virus. The History Channel documentary *Zombies and the Plague* considers the likely spread of a zombie pandemic by recounting the Spanish Flu and Bubonic Plague disasters. And National Geographic's *Zombies: The Truth* imagines a zombie viral pandemic raging out of control and asks whether there is truth behind the zombie myth by examining "the origin of zombies, their religious roots and whether mutated virus strains could cause devastation of zombie proportions. With commentary from zombie enthusiasts and cult experts, virologists and mathematical epidemiologists..."[8]

With these sorts of observations in mind, emergency preparedness consultants are using the threat of zombies to promote their communication tools and emergency planning services.[9] The US Department of Homeland Security paid a consulting firm (via Homeland Security grant) to train military police through a zombie attack drill. Their justification? "The defining characteristics of zombies are that they're unpredictable and resilient. That may be a good way to prepare for what the Pentagon calls asymmetric warfare," according to a defense analyst.[10] And apparently The Centers for Disease Control agrees. They continue to promote a campaign that uses zombie threats to convey public health messages about preparedness.[11]

Researchers have joined the bandwagon as well. Canadian mathematicians have modeled the probability of survival given zombie contagion. They address the likely success from quarantine and cure, and conclude that only rapid, aggressive counter-attacks will protect us from a doomsday scenario.[12] The popular series *TED Talks* includes medical diagnoses of zombification, recommendations on where to go when the apocalypse begins, and even talks *for* zombies on how to survive the humans![13] *The Wall Street Journal* recently reported that college campuses are on the zombie bandwagon and that zombie studies is a viable field of research.[14] The 2014 *International Studies Association* conference includes a mock United Nations Security Council emergency session to discuss a zombie outbreak. Reflecting the relevance of zombies, the agenda for the mock-

UNSC includes international refugee law, pandemics, patent issues, global health crises, and the potential for military action.

So why the attraction? What is the fascination with the undead that has fueled this explosion into all categories of popular culture? And, additionally, what does the change in zombie appeal have to do with the change in our society?

There is a substantial body of literature concluding that we can achieve insights into society and human behavior through the study of pop culture. In Gordon Wright's *Ordeal of Total War, 1939–1945*, which examines the psycho-social consequences of World War II, it is suggested that there are real and identifiable effects of major events on the collective psyche, political structure, social structure, arts, ideas, and intellectual and cultural life. We can learn about ourselves and the consequences of our actions through pop culture. Joseph Gillings's "We're Obsessed with Zombies—Which Says a Lot about Today" highlights that "since at least the late 19th century each generation has created fictional enemies that reflect a broader unease with cultural or scientific developments."[15] Although some iteration of zombies has existed for thousands of years, the modern case of zombies may reflect our specific reactions to what Gillings sees as a "globalised, risk conscious world... [in which] zombies indiscriminately overwhelm states irrespective of wealth, technology and military strength, turning all order to chaos."[16] This reflection of society is important for understanding our underlying fears and motivations. As John Feffer argues in "The Undead and Us," zombies can reflect "how changes in world politics trickle down into our culture. Our dreams represent our anxieties about what's happening in our lives. Our culture represents our anxieties about what's happening in our world."[17]

What do zombies represent?

My first efforts at understanding the growing interest in zombies centered on terrorism as an explanation. In the classic *Night of the Living Dead* (1968) (hereafter *Night*), we encounter a nameless, faceless threat that terrifies us. The main characters are uncertain of the motives of their attackers, who appear to be irrational and illogical in their commitment to destroy us.

The zombies do things we cannot comprehend emotionally or rationally. Their methods are rudimentary but dangerous nonetheless. For some, such as *Night's* Barbra, the fear is paralyzing. She wallows in her fear, and her shock leads to a near-comatose state that leaves her vulnerable. Without the help of Ben she would surely succumb to the zombies, just as her brother did.[18]

Ben's behavior suggests that the key is preparation. He reinforces vulnerable spots, fortifies entry points, takes stock of his resources, and gathers the necessary equipment. He develops a plan for responding to attacks, and identifies an escape route. His actions reveal that even though we cannot reverse the threat, we can protect and prepare ourselves from specific attacks and imminent danger, and we can be preemptive in reducing vulnerabilities.

Cooperation in this effort becomes a center-point of the plot when characters emerge from the basement and propose a strategy of isolationism. The five in the basement, and in particular Harry Cooper, believe that their safety is best ensured by withdrawing from the threat. Ben determines that the basement is a "deathtrap" and he devises a plan to escape the zombie horde and obtain medical care for Harry's daughter Karen, who has been bitten by a zombie. As a result of Ben's actions, all five of the basement-dwelling isolationists are killed by the zombies along with Barbra. Ben hides in the cellar—the strategy he had advocated against—until a posse arrives. Mistaking Ben for a zombie, they shoot and kill him and he is burned alongside the zombie bodies.

Night marks a critical juncture in the evolution of the zombie film. Although it was produced with a minimal budget of $115,000, in recent years it has received critical acclaim and was selected by the Library of Congress in 1999 for preservation in the National Film Registry as a film deemed "culturally, historically or aesthetically significant." The movie's themes continue to resonate with fans of the horror film genre, and more generally with mainstream audiences. To add to Browning's discussion in this volume, according to George A. Romero *Night* is based on the theme of revolution developed in Matheson's *I Am Legend*:

> I thought *I Am Legend* was about revolution. I said if you're going to do something about revolution, you should start at the beginning. I mean, Richard starts his book with one man left; everybody in the world has become a vampire... I don't care what they are. I don't care where they came from. They could be any disaster. They could be an earthquake, a hurricane, whatever. They don't represent, in my mind, anything except a global change of some kind. And the stories are about how people respond or fail to respond to this. That's really all they've ever represented to me. In Richard's book, in the original *I Am Legend*, that's what I thought that book was about. There's this

global change and there's one guy holding out saying, wait a minute, I'm still a human. He's wrong. Go ahead. Join them. You'll live forever! In a certain sense he's wrong but on the other hand, you've got to respect him for taking that position. Zombies to me don't represent anything in particular. They are a global disaster that people don't know how to deal with.[19]

In the post-September 11th world, we can map our fears of terrorism and our efforts at counterterrorism onto the zombie attacks that occur in the movie. But the metaphor breaks down upon closer examination. First, the symbolism does not work temporally. Although there is a clear increase in zombie interest following the terrorist events of September 11, 2001, movies such as *Night* predate the concern with terrorism. Arguably, the fear and fascination with the spread of communism provides a better metaphor for movies such as *Night* and the *Invasion of the Body Snatchers*. This raises a second problem: although we can identify themes relevant to terrorism in *Night*, we can also identify these themes in robot movies, alien attack stories, superhero genres, and other niche films. If we are to understand the unique growth of our zombie fascination, we need to identify a specific connection to the zombie subgenre that does not extend into films about giant robots, aliens, and other threats to human existence (see Figure 3.1).

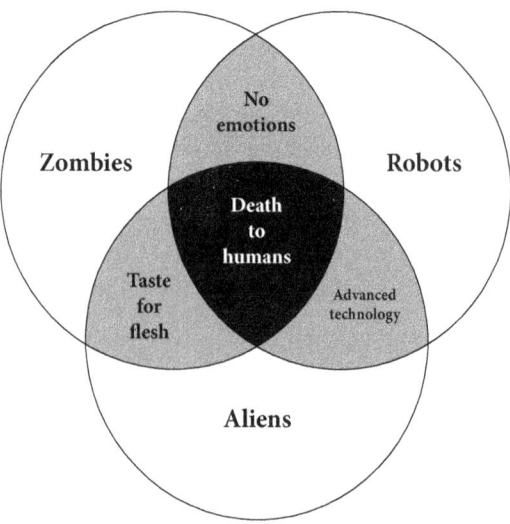

FIGURE 3.1   *Representing the zombie/robot/alien distinction*

Finally, other metaphors seem equally valid when applied to the zombie subgenre. The list of explanations for what the zombies represent is lengthy and diverse:

- Communism
- National socialism
- Consumerism
- The result of "a good deal of anger, mostly that the 60's didn't work"—Romero
- Because people have given up hope
- Coping with the aftermath of World War II
    - Attempts to make sense of life in the absence of ethical and philosophical frameworks that were shattered by the war's violence
- Confronting a(n) (atheistic) fear of the dead
- AIDS
- A reaction to Republican rule in the United States (Wasik and Murphy, 2012)[20]
- The sexuality of teenage boys (while vampires represent the sexuality of teenage girls)
- Fascination with "abomination"
- An excuse for bloodshed

All are viable, interesting explanations, but I propose an alternative—one that provides a deeper connection to the zombie apocalypse, and that better explains why we care so much about it.

Apocalyptic globalization

In 2000, Robert D. Kaplan forecasted a "Coming Anarchy" of environmental scarcity, weapons proliferation, disintegrating borders, and clashing civilizations.[21] The growing problems of poverty, plague, famine—all evident in subsections of Africa—were combining with the transformative aspects of globalization to create instability and chaos. This was not surprising in parts of the world where governments and social institutions were underdeveloped. But, Kaplan warned, it is only a matter of time before this same anarchy threatens the West.

One could extend Kaplan's argument and suggest that the unintended consequences of globalization threaten social, political, and economic systems both within and across states. Globalization begins with advancements to communication and transportation technologies, which extend across borders and generate new public demands. Individuals are deprived, and recognize this deprivation because of the information they have received through globalization's exchanges. They want more, and force their governments to respond. Leaders are then left with the choice of repressing demands or using legitimate or illegitimate means to satisfy the demands of their populations. International trade is the most likely outcome, which in turn fuels greater market efficiency, powers innovations in technology, and restarts the cycle of interdependence.

In a groundbreaking work from 1972, scientists used computer modeling to forecast the trends of world population, industrialization, pollution, food production, and resource depletion. They discovered the *Limits to Growth*: that collapse of the global economy and precipitous population decline were likely, by 2030, if current trends continued.[22] What is particularly disturbing about this research is that a 2008 study confirmed that the real-world data since 1972 is almost identical to the models presented in *Limits*.[23] In other words, we are on a trajectory that is unsustainable, and that may have devastating global consequences.

The effects of unchecked consumption are only one troubling aspect of globalization, but they highlight a particularly important dimension. Individually, we may acknowledge a problem with the direction of globalization. And we may choose to "think globally, act locally." But in truth we are dealing with an extremely complicated and multi-dimensional phenomenon that we are ill-equipped to comprehend, never mind to affect. We feel powerless to evoke the kind of change that will save Emperor penguins or reverse global warming or repair the ozone layer. We cannot just recycle and fix everything. In fact, even if we were to reduce our individual carbon footprint to negligible levels, it would not matter on a global scale.

The "Tragedy of the Commons" (1968) explained that common resources—such as the oceans, the atmosphere, space—require unique cooperative protective agreements that are extremely difficult to enact and enforce.[24] This is because the profits from these common resources are gained exclusively by the exploiter, while the costs of exploiting are shared by everyone.

Consequently, as human populations increase there will be increasing pressure on finite (and especially common) resources at both the local and global levels. The ultimate result is overexploitation and ruin. Sustainability is not likely because common resources can be exploited by anyone who can assert their right to do so.

We don't have to know the science behind these unintended consequences of globalization to realize they are there. The anecdotes and allusions to the pressures of globalization portend earth's doom. Examples abound: the satellite imagery of melting polar ice caps, warnings about the waste products that come from bottled water, and so forth. Even *Rolling Stone* magazine has weighed in on the environmental mess with "Global Warming's Terrifying New Math," an article that spells out the failures of the Copenhagen agreement and the unsustainability of our current path of fossil fuel consumption.[25]

As if this environmental muddle were not enough to generate a sense of despair, the unintended consequences of globalization also extend into conflict, economic exploitation, and political instability. Environmental scarcity actually leads to war, according to Thomas Homer-Dixon, who identifies resource competition as a primary cause of civil war.[26] But globalization has also facilitated small arms proliferation through black marketers who are more mobile, better able to communicate, and more responsive to demand as a result of improvements to technology. As a result of globalization, ideas and resources spread. *Doctors Without Borders* is an example on the "good will" side of the ledger—experts with access to medicines and health care can get these to the people who need them most. But ideas about how to shoot up a school also spread and capture the imaginations of individuals who might not otherwise have been inclined to resort to violence.

Furthermore, tools of violence have been democratized. Individuals have access to weapons of mass-killing that traditionally have been under the exclusive control of states. As Martin Van Creveld argues in the *Democratization of War*, this results in groups and individuals posing a greater threat to populations than ever before.[27]

We also increasingly see the predatory consequences of economic inequality. A mentality of economic "survival of the fittest" in an era of globalization has led to a growing gap between the richest and poorest—one that is unsustainable.

All of this information is available to us at the push of a button, on a hand-held device that we carry with us everywhere. We may even be wearing Google's new neck tattoo that authorizes our hands-free perpetual access to the World Wide Web so that we can order that package through Amazon.com that will be delivered by an unmanned drone. The information and the possibilities may be exciting, but they are also overwhelming. We suffer from *information glut*: a paralyzing overabundance of information that requires expertise to wade through and to interpret.

On an individual level, we may be paralyzed by the reality of globalization. Collectively, we suffer from an ingenuity gap. Homer-Dixon argues that the complexity, the pace, and often the unpredictability of events in our world are soaring.[28] If we are to meet the challenges we face in this new world, we need more ingenuity. But we cannot always supply the ingenuity we need at the right times and places because we suffer from cognitive overload, inadequate knowledge, time lags between needing to know and knowing, and an inadequacy of experts capable of supplying the innovations and solutions to the many problems that are being generated by globalization. The unintended consequences do not necessarily outweigh the benefits of globalization, but they require a combination of time, innovation, and expertise to overcome, and in many cases that combination is not available.

Kaplan's *Coming Anarchy* interpreted these unintended consequences as leading to a breakdown of society. But it is notable that states are breaking down too. Moises Naim, in the "5 Wars of Globalization" (2004), highlights that globalization has empowered agile, stateless, resourceful networks that engage in illegal trade in drugs, arms, intellectual property, people, and money.[29] Governments have responded with a collection of wars: the War on Terror, War on Drugs, and so forth. But, Naim argues, governments are going to lose these wars unless they can adopt new strategies to deal with a larger, unprecedented struggle that now shapes the world as much as confrontations between nation-states once did.

The result is states that are failing. There are many examples in current events, such as Sudan and Afghanistan. Many others are on the precipice.[30] Even seemingly secure nation-states such as Ukraine are a few events away from collapse, fracture, and (civil) war.

The key to overcoming the challenges of globalization may be cross-border cooperation, mobility, and information acquisition and sharing. But all of these require solutions to the *Ingenuity Gap*. And with each new problem that emerges from globalization, states lag behind in providing timely solutions that serve collective needs.

The parallel to zombies[31]

Some have argued that globalization is a culmination of a global transformative process that traces back to the emergence of capitalism. As Castillo contends in this volume, monsters represent the consequences of human trespasses of the natural, social, and moral orders. And we can situate throughout stories about monsters the vestiges of the emergence of capitalism, colonialism, slavery, the establishment and refining of global markets, and globalization. If indeed the "progress of human technology" can produce "cataclysmic byproduct[s]," then zombies, as Castillo rightly contends, may be as evolutionary as they are politically *re*volutionary (see, for example, Browning's chapter in this volume). Feffer describes the link between zombies and this amalgamation of global processes as follows:

> Our fascination with zombies is partly a transposed fear of immigration (which the departed Ugly Americans series riffed on), of China displacing the United States as the world's top economy, of bots taking over our computers, of financial markets that can melt down in a single morning. Zombies overwhelm local control, state control, national control, and ultimately international control. Like globalization, they are an uncontainable and voracious force.[32]

In the process of globalization, as well as in the zombie apocalypse, one can argue a sense of inevitable destruction and impending doom. In both cases, there is no easy solution. Neither phenomenon is controlled or managed by anyone. There is no leader, no "man behind the curtain," no one calling the shots. Globalization is led by the "invisible hand" of the market—the "imperatives" of consumption and homogenization. Benjamin Barber describes it in this manner:

> [globalization] is being borne in on us by the onrush of economic and ecological forces that demand integration and uniformity and that mesmerize the world with fast music, fast computers, and fast food—with MTV, Macintosh, and McDonald's, pressing nations into one commercially homogenous global network: one McWorld tied together by technology, ecology, communications, and commerce.[33]

For Kaplan, it is an anarchic process with no central authority and burgeoning chaos.

And, although there is no one in control, that doesn't mean that we do not share culpability for the outcomes. There is a notable theme in zombie media that in some small way we have contributed to the plague that will lead to our demise. In *28 Days Later* it is the scientist who ignores proper safety protocols. In Max Brooks's book *World War Z*, the failure of governments to act swiftly and to share information and resources leads to the rapid spread of the plague. *I Am Legend* alludes to a thermonuclear war as the cause. M. Keith Booker's *Monsters, Mushroom Clouds, and the Cold War: American Science Fiction and the Roots of Postmodernism, 1946–1964* posits that a primary lesson of the nuclear era is that scientific progress is not a panacea for human suffering and that technological advances can stimulate social anxiety. Instead, humans not only contribute to, but are the root of, the problem.[34]

Barber conceptualizes globalization as a similar process in that there is no democratic voice in the *McWorld*, but we fuel it through our purchases. We accept it because of the attraction of accessibility and the pleasure of purchasing:

> McWorld does manage to look pretty seductive in a world obsessed with Jihad. It delivers peace, prosperity, and relative unity—if at the cost of independence, community, and identity (which is generally based on difference). The primary political values required by the global market are order and tranquility, and freedom—as in the phrases "free trade," "free press," and "free love." Human rights are needed to a degree, but not citizenship or participation—and no more social justice and equality than are necessary to promote efficient economic production and consumption.[35]

Zombies are driven by a cannibalistic urge. In some stories they thirst for brains, in others human flesh. But their drive is primordial, mindless, and never-ending. In "Dead Right," a short story by Geoffrey Landis, a boxer faces a zombie opponent and recognizes that he cannot match the will of an undead pugilist:

> He didn't seem to notice any of my blows, though I was landing three for every one he hit me with. My hands were beginning to hurt. I was sweating rivers, but he hadn't started to sweat at all... he was wearing me down. The combinations I used had been optimized and fine-tuned and should have been able to knock over a horse, but he kept on moving.[36]

The threat is never-ending because "how can you knock out a fighter who's *already dead*?" The same theme is evident in *World War Z* (2006), where the recognition of the absolute and final nature of the apocalyptic threat is overwhelming:

For the first time in history, we faced an enemy that was actively waging total war. They had no limits of endurance. They would never negotiate, never surrender. They would fight until the very end because, unlike us, every single one of them, every second of every day, was devoted to consuming all life on Earth. That's the kind of enemy that was waiting for us...[37]

Barber's description of globalization includes "imperatives": a market imperative, a resource imperative, an information-technology imperative, and an ecological imperative. As he describes it, "by shrinking the world and diminishing the salience of national borders, these imperatives have in combination achieved a considerable victory over factiousness and particularism, and not least of all over their most virulent traditional form—nationalism."[38] These necessities of globalization transform the world as we know it, while they reinforce and necessitate their existence. They are what Browning describes in this volume as the insurmountable "multiple threat." As they take hold, individuality is lost and the collective horde gains traction.

Earlier versions of zombie stories included voodoo masters and slave-drivers who poisoned their undead and controlled them. But with the advent of the zombie plague apocalypse, from Romero's *Night of the Living Dead* in 1968, "it suddenly became clear that no one was running the show. No spooky witch doctor. No creepy guy with a skinny little moustache and a Hypno-Wheel. No social contract. And seemingly, no God."[39]

A third theme to emerge between the apocalypses of globalization and zombies: there is no moral framework or rationality. Marx and Engels offer a prescient description of globalization when they describe capitalist expansion as ruthless and inevitable:

> The bourgeoisie, by the rapid improvement of all instruments of production, by the immensely facilitated means of communication, draws all, even the most barbarian, nations into civilization. The cheap prices of its commodities are the heavy artillery with which it batters down all Chinese walls, with which it forces the barbarians' intensely obstinate hatred of foreigners to capitulate. It compels all nations, on pain of extinction, to adopt the bourgeois mode of production; it compels them to introduce what it calls civilization into their midst, i.e., to become bourgeois themselves. In one word, it creates a world after its own image.[40]

As both Browning and Castillo allude to in this volume, zombies can be seen as the "anti-productive" forces that consume without producing. They are unsustainable, unintended consequences of capitalism and globalization, and their outcomes are illogical yet inevitable. In this sense they are horrific monsters that give us no choice but to resort to the zero point "state of nature."

In the zombie apocalypse the social contract is out the door as governments kill citizens in order to attempt to stem the tide of the contagion. There is seemingly no calculation beyond the "kill or be killed" survivalist mentality. The rule of law ceases to exist. There is no sense of right or wrong, just empty vessels subject to an invisible hand guiding them. There is anarchy and there is the state of nature.

Apocalyptic contagion

The similarities may exist, and globalization may be a compelling source of the zombie metaphor, but this still doesn't explain why we are so interested in the zombie phenomenon. Many important events and trends fail to capture our attention or generate spin-off multi-billion dollar horror genres. Why do we care so much about zombies?

To answer this, I consider the underlying process of mass zombification and globalization: diffusion. Diffusion is a standard concept in social (and natural) science research, and involves regular and identifiable patterns of spreading ideas, innovations, and physical processes. Of notable importance is that a diffusion process has predictable temporal and spatial characteristics as the subject of analysis spreads out, or moves from a region of high concentration to regions of lower concentration. It is possible to map the spread of a particular innovation or phenomenon and to generate predictions about its future spread. It is also possible to learn about the phenomenon being diffused by examining its spread.

The diffusion process, simply put, involves the flow of some phenomenon—be it informational, behavioral, or biological. However, diffusion is not the only form of flow. Spatial interactions are another class of movements which involve the flows which are essential to the normal functioning of an existing structure of relations. In contrast to interactions, diffusion involves the movements which alter those structures. In this sense, diffusion is a distinct type of flow which transforms the existing landscape.

How does this matter for the zombie apocalypse or for globalization? If we can make sense of the structures into which these phenomena are introduced, we can consider how those structures are changed by the phenomenon, or how the structures facilitate or inhibit the spread of the phenomenon. Or, we can determine what it is about the decision-makers within those structures that make them more likely to be attracted to the phenomenon. Put in simpler terms, we can determine how globalization processes interact with the international landscape: how globalization is modified over time, how the landscape is modified, and how it is accepted or rejected by people with specific characteristics.[41] We can also determine, by looking at zombie movies and literature, how zombification spreads and is repelled. This can be a function of determinants such as the landscape, the susceptibility of the human population, the abilities of zombies, and the extent to which leaders or agents manage the process of spread.

Among the most highly regarded studies of diffusion are those advanced by Torsten Hagerstrand (1967), Lawrence Brown (1981) and Everett Rogers (1985). Hagerstrand defines the diffusion of innovations simply as "the origin and dissemination of cultural novelties."[42] According to Brown, the distributional characteristics associated with a phenomenon "change over time, rather than remaining static, and the process by which such change occurs, that is, by which innovations spread from one locale or one social group to another, is called diffusion."[43] Rogers, a pioneer in the study of diffusion processes in sociology, defined diffusion as "communication of information under uncertainty; 'diffusion is the process by which an innovation is communicated through certain channels, over time, among members of a social system.'"[44] A more general definition conceives of diffusion as "a process by which behavior or characteristics of the landscape change as a result of what happens elsewhere earlier. Spatial diffusion is the spread of the phenomenon, over space and time, from limited origins."[45]

The common elements to these definitions are important to understanding the dynamics of diffusion. Each conceptualization addresses the components of (1) a phenomenon, (2) which is transferred in some particular manner, (3) over time, (4) to a particular receiver, (5) across a specific landscape. The particular manner of transfer may be through an entity that *promotes* or guides the process, or it may be a self-diffusing phenomenon. The particulars of the elements themselves are important to understanding how the process of diffusion unfolds. These characteristics affect the spatial and temporal diffusion patterns of phenomena as similar (or diverse) as globalization and mass zombification.

Globalization is all about diffusion. It has been defined as processes leading to international interconnectedness, including increasing flows of trade, investment, and communication.[46] Research on the diffusion of globalization abounds, and addresses each of the components listed above. Diffusion analyses have aided our understanding of political globalization such as the diffusion of democratic processes. It has clarified the facilitators and barriers to economic globalization in various parts of the world. And it has helped to explain cultural transformations through communication, transportation, and exchange over borders.

To study how mass zombification diffuses, we should begin with the phenomenon of zombification.

Phenomenon and channel: zombification through virus

The process of zombification varies from story to story. In folklore, it often involved sleepwalking humans who were either hypnotized or poisoned, then subjected to slavery by a master. The films *The Cabinet of Dr. Caligari* (1920) and *White Zombie* (1932) fit this mold of a voodoo-based transformation with a controlling "witch doctor" who manipulates the victim. In the 1950s, a series of movies such as *Invasion of the Body Snatchers* (1956) depicted aliens resurrecting and reanimating corpses or comatose victims in order to utilize them for nefarious purposes. The "zombies" were puppeted and instructed to do the bidding of otherworldly masters.

In more recent iterations, and in particular following Romero's *Night*, the zombification process generally involves a channel of transmission whereby blood-borne pathogens are passed through a bite or infection in open wounds. As such, it has been compared to rabies or a mutant measles strain. Generally, there is no cure, and to limit the spread a zombie's brain must be destroyed. These "infection narratives" involve virus pandemics that lead to relentlessly aggressive hordes of undead who invade and destroy indiscriminately. If globalization reveals processes whereby traditions are torn apart and our cultural and historical fabrics of social interaction are destroyed, zombies mimic this carnage through their flesh-eating. There is no negotiation or reasoning with the impulses wrought by these biological infections, only terrifying attempts to escape and avoid the plague-spreading monsters.

The cause of the pandemic varies from story to story; however, in most cases it is the result of human experimentation and technological advancement gone awry. *Resident Evil's* T-virus stems from biological weapons. Romero's *Night* hints that the pandemic is stimulated by radioactive contamination from a space probe that was deliberately exploded in Earth's atmosphere when radiation was detected. *28 Days Later* involves a chimpanzee, infected with a rage-inducing virus, attacking scientists and animal activists attempting to free the animal. These examples suggest a criticism of human attempts to control processes and phenomena that we do not understand. Our limited scientific expertise generates vulnerabilities as we unleash nature in the interest of human progress.

> *Observations*: The evolution of how zombification occurs is about a transition from agency to biological necessity. Early versions of zombies were created by evil slave masters or alien schemers who sought to control, manipulate, and transform mankind. In the modern iterations of the infection narratives, we see a process that is unmanaged, spreads rapidly, diffuses to all corners of the earth, and mimics the most destructive pandemics of history. They spread as an inevitable and undiscerning biological imperative. Thus, the appeal of zombification is in part due to its realism: we see the spread of ebola, bird flu, swine flu, HIV, and recognize the possibility of a zombie plague. And we are ultimately responsible for these viral pandemics that rage out of control as we attempt to modify nature in the interest of science, progress, and profit.

Agent: zombie

The agent of transmission is the zombie itself, a monster that varies drastically. Some are dead, others are barely living. Some feast on flesh, others drink blood, many eat brains. Some exhibit super-human strength and speed while others are weak, shambling, and literally falling to pieces. Some speak. Some feel. Some learn. Some have self-awareness.

In general, a zombie is capable of some remembered behavior. Its bite will lead to violent illness and death. It feeds on the living. It has been reanimated after death, or exists in an undead state. Destroying the brain will destroy the zombie.

The extent of the zombie's mental capacity is often a tool for satirical reflection on the distinction between "normal" humans who engage in mindless action and behavior, and the undead who contemplate. In some cases the zombie is slow and dim-witted, if at all sentient (*World*

War Z—the book). In others zombies use simple tools.[47] Some display evidence of learning and cognitive processing.[48] Extreme examples of this include zombies in *Re-Animator* and *Day of the Dead* who appear (intentionally) more reflective and self-aware than their human counterparts.

In some cases, we see rudimentary cooperation among the zombies. The film version of *World War Z* (2011) involves zombie collective action, motivated by some unclear and unspoken impetus. They work together to climb walls, enter buildings, and overturn cars. Their numbers are incredible and coordinated, and they attack in waves of undead flesh that is undistinguishable as individuals. In some ways they are notably more organized than the panicking and ineffectual humans attempting to flee the pandemic.

The speed of the zombie is an important distinction. Romero's movies reveal a shambling and slow zombie that affords the victim the time to contemplate his or her own death. Zombies can be slow enough to run away from (as in the *World War Z* and *I Am Legend* books) or they can be fast enough to give serious pursuit to a sprinting human (as in the *World War Z* and *I Am Legend* movies). Faster zombies portend the inevitable death that we cannot escape and the escalation of the threat to a level that no individual can overcome.

> *Observations*: There is no single conception of a zombie, although the commonalities reveal an undead threat that is unyielding, continuous, potentially adaptive, and formidable. Moreover, the threat in many ways resembles us. On the outside, other than the rotting flesh, they can appear to be our sister, father, friend, boss, or daughter. Inside they are gone, now motivated purely by biological necessity. In most instances the zombies are not nameless and faceless enemies, but instead they are the people we see every day—which suggests that the monstrous potential is inside all of us and all around us.

(Unwilling) receiver: us

The individuals to whom the phenomenon is transferred have lost the battle. They quickly become the agent, and are killed or become the diffusers. Those who do survive in the movies represent a broad cross-section of society. In *28 Days Later* they are angry young women, post-coma patients, fathers and daughters, and military renegades. This would not suggest that the survival of the fittest is the determinant of survivors. Instead, the characters seem to represent randomness that is not attributable to individual characteristics. Put differently, the zombie story is rarely about the exceptionalism of the survivor. It is instead about the process of surviving. Survivors do everything they can to stave off death. They shoot the zombie that was once their fiancée. They mind their own business until the plague descends upon them, then they are willing to take matters into their own hands to escape the biological infection. But they are not super-human. It is rarely the case that exceptional ingenuity makes the difference between life and undeath. And it is unusual that humans are able to organize on a large scale to respond collectively to the zombie threat. The survivors are average, fearful, determined individuals who deny, however temporarily, the apparently inevitable fate of all humans.

Observations: Survival appears to be random and depends on individual chance. This, in and of itself, may be part of the appeal of the zombie genre: that any of us could survive. The unwilling receiver of zombification has the opportunity and ability to determine their own fate, however dire the circumstances may be.

Landscape: local context and factors

The landscape and the characteristics of the environment can serve to facilitate or inhibit the spread of zombification. The greater the population density, the greater the likelihood of a quickly growing horde of zombies. Communal spaces are also conducive to easier movement, identification of and access to potential victims. Accordingly, most zombie films take place in cities and urban centers. In contrast, rural areas would provide hiding spaces, fewer zombies roaming, and fewer indications of potential victims. Unless attacking zombies are sensitive to smell or sight, the odds of transmission would be reduced. But once the initial massive spread of zombies occurs, the natural progression is for the horde to diffuse into the countryside. *28 Weeks Later* exemplifies this; many of the most suspenseful scenes take place in rural settings where zombies happen upon the humans seeking refuge.

Mountainous regions and uneven ground would affect the movement of shambling zombies. Whether zombies are capable of moving across (or under) water would determine whether islands are likely to be locales of zombification. Of course, once an infection reaches an island, the ability of potential victims to escape may also be reduced. Forestation may improve the chances of escape if zombies are unable to climb, or if they have limited ability to identify hiding spots. A zombie's problem-solving skills can be put to the test by the rare human who is clever in sheltering and uses the terrain to their advantage.

Preparation certainly affects the prospect of withstanding zombie attacks and invasion. Well-defended areas may withstand a siege for periods of time; the ability of zombies to wait out starving or thirsty potential victims may determine whether fortresses are effective strategies against the zombie horde. Weapons can also make a positive difference if the wielders are capable of head shots and repelling onslaughts through combat; this is often the most critical determinant of success in zombie and horror-themed survival video games such as *Resident Evil*. Wealth is conducive to preparation; it would stand to reason that wealthier communities would be more likely to have resources available in the midst of an apocalypse. That said, preparation and equipment is irrelevant if the humans panic. Hysteria can undermine the best-laid plans.

> *Observations*: Although the landscape can affect the interplay between humans and zombies, the characteristics of the zombies themselves are critical for determining whether the landscape facilitates or inhibits the zombification. The extent to which barriers can deter or eliminate the zombie threat depends on the ability of the zombie to reason, adapt, and react as well as the ability of the humans to use these barriers effectively. The distance across which zombies must travel to infect humans will affect the speed and likelihood of the spread. However, that spread is also a function of the coordination among zombies, and the communication by humans. In most zombie stories, human communication systems break down and individual humans are frequently unable to organize. Accordingly, independent of other determinants, the landscape is not a sufficient explanation for the appeal of the zombie genre.

Promotion: leaders and controlling entities

Promotion is often cited in diffusion research as the most useful determinant of a pattern of spread. This is because we can better anticipate the likely pattern if we know the interests of the promoter. Take, for example, the promotion of democracy abroad. Knowing that the United States has been a strong (vocal) advocate of democratic change in the world, we can anticipate where democratization would be likely to occur based on where the US wants democracy to happen, the cost the US is willing to pay, the tools the US has available to bring about democratic change, and so forth.

But what is particularly notable about the zombie subgenre, since *Night* and *I Am Legend* four decades later, is the lack of promoters. In this modern era there are no advocates for zombification. There are very few international entities capable of affecting the spread of zombies (note the ineffectiveness of the United Nations in *World War Z*)—thus the apocalypse. The plague is typically motivated by biological infection, not by any external intent.

In contrast, the stories of the 1950s and earlier involved some level of promotion. Aliens reanimated dead humans to take over the world. Alchemists and practitioners of black magic used voodoo, hypnosis, and poisonous potions to create obedient and submissive slaves. These were not the rotting corpses of the modern zombie apocalypse; rather they were laborers and sleepwalkers that served their masters dutifully.

The inception of the modern zombie apocalypse is often attributable to an individual or entity. It is the corporation in pursuit of profits that disregards moral considerations and safety procedures in the interest of money-making discoveries. It is the government that neglects popular opinion and produces biological weapons. It is the superpower that ignores the dangers of radiation in order to win the space race. It is the scientist that is blinded by the pursuit of technological advance and ignores the ethical dilemmas embedded in scientific progress. But these catalysts do not control the zombie apocalypse. More often, it is the loss of control of their advancements to nature and natural processes that results in the spread of the virus. It is the unintended consequences of their pursuits that unleash the apocalyptic scenarios.

Once the apocalypse has begun, its most notable feature is its uncontrollability. The Zombie Research Society, a tongue-in-cheek website that connects current events to the zombie craze, includes a research note on the "Worst Country for Zombie Survival."[49] They highlight population density and authoritarianism as the best determinants for survival, noting that natural disasters are not mitigated in countries with high population density and dictatorial regimes. With this in mind, they conclude that India and China are the worst places to find yourself during a zombie outbreak.

However, this highlights an important aspect of the zombie apocalypse: no governments survive! States no longer exist in the vast majority of zombie films and books.[50] They fail to respond adequately to the massive threat and collapse under the weight of the zombie crisis. Given their inability to control the impending disaster, they lose control of their population. The rule of law breaks down, and the state no longer functions.

What does this mean? Recognize that the central purpose of a state is to provide security to its collective citizenry. As Hobbes described in Leviathan, individuals give up the "right to all things" in order to be secure. Although the state of nature affords us the right to kill, the right to take and use any resource we choose, life in the state of nature is "…and which is worst of all, continual fear, and danger of violent death; and the life of man, solitary, poor, nasty, brutish, and short."[51] As soon as we gain from others, we become a target. We accumulate, and distinguish ourselves as someone worth killing. As a result, we ultimately are willing to give up the right to all things to the government, which guarantees our (collective) protection in exchange for being able to set the rules.

With regard to modern zombies, there is no promotion, no agency, no mechanism. The zombie apocalypse is, as Neville observes in *I Am Legend*, "a product of science gone awry or nature's revenge on runaway human growth."[52] No one guarantees our protection during the apocalypse. In fact, the only solutions states employ in order to stem the tide of zombification are mass killing and deserting large segments of the population to their attackers.

States collapse under the strain of a zombie apocalypse because they attempt to maintain the pretext of control. They ignore the threats, reject the need for immediate and decisive action, and refuse to acknowledge that the public is in danger. Especially in democratic societies, the government's desire to maintain the support of the citizenry outweighs the need to apply the tourniquet. This is evident in *World War Z*:

> What, you would have rather we told people the truth? That it wasn't a new strain of rabies but a mysterious uber-plague that reanimated the dead? Can you imagine the panic that would have happened: the protest, the riots, the billions in damage to private property? Can you imagine all those wet-pants senators who would have brought the government to a standstill so they could railroad some high-profile and ultimately useless "Zombie Protection Act" through Congress? Can you imagine the damage it would have done to that administration's political capital? We're talking about an election year, and a damn hard, uphill fight.[53]

For all intents and purposes, states cease to exist during the zombie apocalypse. Individuals are required to rely upon themselves for survival.

Rules no longer apply, and laws are suspended or aborted. We return to the state of nature, and once again have the "right to all things." In *Monster Island, A Zombie Novel*, the back cover warns, "It's one month after a global disaster. The most 'developed' nations of the world have fallen to the shambling zombie masses. Only a few pockets of humanity survive."[54] The back cover to *The Beginning of the End (Apocalypse Z)* similarly warns, "Governments scramble to stop the zombie virus, people panic, so-called Safe Havens are established, the world erupts into chaos; soon it's every man, woman, and child for themselves."[55]

> *Observations*: There is an appeal to regaining the "right to all things." In a world where the pursuit of progress has let us down and unleashed a relentlessly aggressive pandemic upon us, we are unable (and potentially unwilling) to rely on anyone or anything but ourselves. Science, technology, capitalism, or the power of our government has let us down and resulted in cataclysmic events that leave us vulnerable and on the brink of undeath.[56] Holding destiny in our hands, realizing that the government we distrust is no longer in control of us leaves us (1) terrified, and (2) empowered to determine our own future. This is certainly reason to be fascinated with the zombie apocalypse! As one enlightened character realizes, "There has to be a better way, a middle path where we take responsibility for our own protection."[57]

Reconnecting zombies and globalization

As the zombie apocalypse descends upon us, our governments fail and we become the ultimate controllers of our destiny. We are not prepared for this. Years of subservience, conformity, rule-abiding social interaction, and lethargy have created an impression and, as a result, few will survive.

But rules no longer apply and we are suddenly empowered with choice—real choice. Morality is irrelevant in the state of nature. We resort to a Machiavellian set of principles, including *"might makes right"* and *"the end justifies the means."* Such principles may seem abhorrent when applied to modern society but are perfectly reasonable in the midst of an apocalypse. This means that we can choose to leave our wife behind, without guilt, when she dilly dallies as Alice did in *28 Weeks Later*. It is our choice as to how best to survive, and the only judgment that matters is whether we succeeded in outlasting the undead, and in avoiding a contagious bite.

Note that the absence of the state is unique to the zombie subgenre. As the apocalypse descends as a result of asteroids, aliens, robots, the future "us," diseases, or apes, the state is there to fight for us. In fact, in *Independence Day*, it is the president in his fighter jet who helps to deal the death blow to the mother ship. The government is there, in almost all of those cases, to save the day or to give its best effort to retain authority and social control.

And this is the irony of both the zombie subgenre and globalization. With both approaching apocalypses, we sense the impending doom and the breakdown of the institutions that we have come to rely upon. The zombies are closing in everywhere and threatening to eat us. They are an insatiable horde, gorging their way through the remaining living. In the process they destroy social structure and order, leaving chaos and anarchy. Globalization is devouring the world's resources and turning every corner of the planet into a homogenized version of McWalmart. And yet, *these phenomena simultaneously empower us!*

As a result of globalization's technology and communication advancements, we have more information than ever before. And information is power; we need only look to the examples of the Arab Spring to see how networked individuals can coordinate social movements and dissent in order to bring about fundamental change. Technology has the potential to decentralize and democratize, and with these changes a state can become obsolete, leaving us to choose our own path and our own rules. It may not result in the complete breakdown of the state (yet?), but it certainly empowers non-state actors and forces states to adapt to new threats.[58]

This is the attraction: In spite of an apocalypse, we become the powerful and we hold our survival in our own hands. We control our destiny. To survive, we must become Machiavellian in our calculations. But we have the ability to determine the course of events and to use coercion to shape our future. This is distinct from social reality as we know it—the evolution of the international state system has largely been defined by the centralization of authority (in the form of states) and the disarming of non-state actors.[59] In fact, an international norm that has increasingly taken hold accepts that governments are the only entities that may use violence legitimately.

In this new post-apocalyptic world, we can use force. We can be brutal, anarchistic, animalistic; in fact, we may choose to model nature and act animalistically, for animals may serve to be our best defense. As National Wildlife Federation naturalist David Mizejewski suggests, "if there was ever a zombie uprising, wildlife would kick its ass" because "zombies are essentially walking carrion, and Mother Nature doesn't let anything go to waste."[60] Birds would scavenge on the carcasses, mammals would dismember the bodies, and decomposers would feed off any remaining flesh. We would do well to mimic behavior in the state of nature, and to rely on our ruthless and brutal survival instincts.

It may be difficult to return to the state of nature, to destroy human-looking foes. On the other hand, the idea of unrestricted liberty (what Hobbes called the "right to all things") may grow on us. We may enjoy the challenge of the undead, and the ability to use any means necessary to ensure our survival. As John Skipp observes, "The endless useful permutations of the walking dead continue to diversify and beguile because they are us. And nobody really gets tired of looking in a mirror, or marveling at one's own shadow."[61]

Or killing it in bloody, spectacular fashion.

Notes

1. A Google search of "zombie garden gnome" results in no fewer than 219,000 results.
2. *The Week* Staff, "America's $5 Billion Zombie Industry: By the Numbers," *The Week*, October 27, 2011, http://theweek.com/article/index/220774/americas-5-billion-zombie-industry-by-the-numbers; "World War Z," *Box Office Mojo*, accessed September 2, 2015, http://www.boxofficemojo.com/movies/?id=worldwarz.htm.
3. Eddie Makuch, "Resident Evil HD Breaks Sales Records," *GameSpot*, February 9, 2015, http://www.gamespot.com/articles/resident-evil-hd-breaks-sales-records/1100-6425190/.
4. See *Zombie Tools (ZT)*, accessed September 2, 2015, http://www.zombietools.net/.
5. See "Zombie Apocalypse Survival Gear," *True Swords*, accessed September 2, 2015, http://www.trueswords.com/zombie_apocalypse.php.
6. See *Zombie Survival Army-Navy Supplies*, accessed September 2, 2015, http://www.zombiesurvivalorlando.com/.

7   T. E. Sloth and David Wong, "5 Scientific Reasons a Zombie Apocalypse Could Actually Happen," *Cracked*, October 29, 2007, http://www.cracked.com/article_15643_5-scientific-reasons-zombie-apocalypse-could-actually-happen.html#ixzz2yInzMXq7. Note that *Cracked* also reports that, fortunately, such an outbreak would also be likely to fail rapidly. See David Dietle, "7 Scientific Reasons a Zombie Outbreak Would Fail (Quickly)," *Cracked*. August 17, 2010, http://www.cracked.com/article_18683_7-scientific-reasons-zombie-outbreak-would-fail-quickly.html#ixzz2yIoOFiyO.
8   *Zombies: The Truth*, Dir. Mike Wafer (Washington, D.C.: National Geographic Channel, 2010).
9   See, for example, "How Will You Communicate in a Zombie Attack?" *Everbridge*, accessed September 2, 2015, http://www.everbridge.com/how-will-you-communicate-in-a-zombie-attack/?mkt_tok=3RkMMJWWfF9wsRogu67BZKXonjHpfsX56eklW7Hro8Yy0EZ5VunJEUWy20QJTNQ%2FcOedCQkZHblFnVwITq2kT6sNrKcJ.
10 Julie Watson, "'Zombie Apocalypse' Training Drill Organized By Halo Corp. For Military, Police Set For Oct. 31 In San Diego," *Associated Press*, October 27, 2012, http://www.huffingtonpost.com/2012/10/29/zombie-apocalypse-trainining-military-halo-corp-_n_2036996.html.
11 Office of Public Health Preparedness and Response, "Zombie Preparedness," *The Centers for Disease Control and Prevention*, last updated April 10, 2015, http://www.cdc.gov/phpr/zombies.htm.
12 Philip Munz et al., "When Zombies Attack!: Mathematical Modelling of an Outbreak of Zombie Infection," in *Infectious Disease Modelling Research Progress*, ed. Jean Michel Tchuenche and Christinah Chiyaka (New York: Nova Science Publishers, Inc., 2009), 133–50.
13 Tim Verstynen and Bradley Voytek, "Diagnosing a zombie: Brain and body," Ed-Ted, http://ed.ted.com/lessons/diagnosing-a-zombie-tim-verstynen-brad-voytek#review; David Hunter, "How do you decide where to go in a zombie apocalypse?," Ed-Ted, http://ed.ted.com/lessons/how-do-you-decide-where-to-go-in-a-zombie-apocalypse-david-hunter#review; Official Comedy, "DED Talk: A TED Talk For Zombies," YouTube, October 24, 2013, https://www.youtube.com/watch?v=aHxTKj6TdN8.
14 Erica E. Phillips, "Zombie Studies Gain Ground on College Campuses: Students, Professors Study Culture of Living Dead," *Wall Street Journal*, March 3, 2014, http://online.wsj.com/news/articles/SB10001424052702304851104579361451951384512.
15 Joseph Gillings, "We're Obsessed with Zombies—Which Says a Lot About Today," *The Conversation*, February 23, 2015, https://theconversation.com/were-obsessed-with-zombies-which-says-a-lot-about-today-37552.

16 Ibid.
17 John Feffer, "The Undead and Us," *Foreign Policy in Focus*, November 13, 2013, http://fpif.org/undead-us/.
18 This is not the place to debate whether Johnny should have died, deserved to die, or whether I cheered when he was bludgeoned to death.
19 Mariana McConnell, "Interview: George A. Romero on Diary of the Dead," *Cinema Blend*, January 14, 2008, http://www.cinemablend.com/new/Interview-George-A-Romero-On-Diary-Of-The-Dead-7818.html.
20 This idea, according to Bill Wasik and Monica Murphy, made the rounds during the 2008 presidential campaign in the United States...that zombie booms correlated with Republican rule. Romero, after all, had reinvented the genre in the early days of Nixon, and then the Reagan administration ushered in a new wave that included *Re-Animator* and *The Evil Dead*. In Democratic-leaning times, when (so the theory ran) popular rhetoric tends to demonize blood-sucking plutocrats, the Byronic vampire will find himself ascendant; in conservative periods, by contrast, the fear is heaped on mobs of shadowy masses—whether they be criminals or welfare recipients or Muslims—and so zombies naturally rise again to become the undead bugbear of choice.
See Bill Wasik and Monica Murphy, *Rabid: A Cultural History of the World's Most Diabolical Virus* (New York: Penguin Books, 2012), 161.
21 Robert D. Kaplan, *The Coming Anarchy: Shattering the Dreams of the Post Cold War World* (New York: Vintage, 2000).
22 Donella H. Meadows et al., *The Limits to Growth* (New York: Universe Books, 1972).
23 Graham Turner, "A Comparison of 'The Limits to Growth' with Thirty Years of Reality," *Commonwealth Scientific and Industrial Research Organisation (CSIRO)*, CSIRO Working Paper Series 2008–9, Working Paper No. 1834-5638 (June 2008).
24 Garrett Hardin, "The Tragedy of the Commons," *Science* 162, no. 3859 (December 13, 1968): 1243–8.
25 Bill McKibben, "Global Warming's Terrifying New Math," *Rolling Stone Magazine*, July 19, 2012, http://www.rollingstone.com/politics/news/global-warmings-terrifying-new-math-20120719.
26 Thomas Homer-Dixon, *The Ingenuity Gap* (New York: Knopf Publishing, 2000).
27 Martin Van Creveld, *The Transformation of War* (New York: Free Press, 1991).
28 See Homer-Dixon, *The Ingenuity Gap*; and Homer-Dixon, "Environmental Scarcities and Violent Conflict: Evidence from Cases," *International Security* 19, no. 1 (Summer 1994): 5–40.
29 Moises Naim, "5 Wars of Globalization," *Foreign Policy*, January/February 2004, 28–37.

30. FP Staff, "The 2013 Failed States Index—Interactive Map and Rankings," *Foreign Policy (FP)*, June 24, 2013, http://foreignpolicy.com/2013/06/24/the-2013-failed-states-index-interactive-map-and-rankings/.
31. This section emphasizes the post-Romero plague apocalypse rather than the *White Zombie* master/slave dynamic. But one of the most fundamental commonalities between globalization and zombies is that zombies started as slaves (in the *White Zombie* genre) and globalization started with slavery. For a discussion of the latter point, see J.M. Blaut, *The Colonizer's Model of the World: Geographical Diffusionism and Eurocentric History* (New York: Guilford Press, 1993).
32. Feffer, "The Undead and Us."
33. Benjamin Barber, *Jihad vs. McWorld: Terrorism's Challenge to Democracy* (New York: Ballantine Books, 1995), 83.
34. M. Keith Booker, *Monsters, Mushroom Clouds and the Cold War: American Science Fiction and the Roots of Postmodernism, 1946–1964* (Westport, CT: Greenwood Press, 2001).
35. Benjamin R. Barber, "Jihad vs. McWorld," *The Atlantic* (March 1992), http://www.theatlantic.com/magazine/archive/1992/03/jihad-vs-mcworld/303882/.
36. Geoffrey Landis, "Dead Right," in *The Ultimate Zombie*, ed. Byron Preiss and John Betancourt (New York: Dell, 1993), 56.
37. Max Brooks, *World War Z: An Oral History of the Zombie War* (New York: Crown, 2006), 273.
38. Benjamin R. Barber, "Jihad vs. McWorld," *The Atlantic* (March 1992), http://www.theatlantic.com/magazine/archive/1992/03/jihad-vs-mcworld/303882/.
39. John Skipp, *Zombies: Encounters with the Hungry Dead* (New York: Black Dog and Leventhal Publishers, 2009), 14.
40. Karl Marx and Friedrich Engels, *The Communist Manifesto* (New York: Pocket Books, 1964), 65.
41. There are numerous examples of this literature across many social science disciplines. One seminal article is Beth A. Simmons and Zachary Elkins's "The Globalization of Liberalization: Policy Diffusion in the International Political Economy," *American Political Science Review* 98, no. 1 (2004): 171–89.
42. Torsten Hagerstrand, *Innovation Diffusion as a Spatial Process* (Chicago: University of Chicago Press, 1967), 1.
43. Lawrence A. Brown, *Innovation Diffusion: A New Perspective* (New York: Methuen Press, 1981), 1.
44. Everett M. Rogers, *Diffusion of Innovations*, 4th ed. (New York: Free Press, 1985), 5.
45. Richard Morrill, Gary L. Gaile, and Grant Ian Thrall, *Spatial Diffusion* (Newbury Park, CA: Sage Publications, 1988), 7.
46. See Paul Hirst, and Grahame Thompson, "The Future of Globalization," *Cooperation and Conflict: Journal of the Nordic International Studies Association* 37, no. 3 (2002): 247–65.

47 With the first appearance of a "modern, plague" zombie in Romero's *Night of the Living Dead*, the zombie attempts to break a car window using a rock.
48 The main zombie character in Romero's *Dawn of the Dead* realizes the flaw of watching fireworks, and his moment of recognition is a key scene in the film. In *I Am Legend* (2007) a zombie (which admittedly acts more like a vampire than a zombie in many ways) mimics Neville's trap-building and catches him.
49 ZRS Staff, "Worst Country for Zombie Survival," *Zombie Research Society*, February 14, 2012, http://zombieresearchsociety.com/archives/2606.
50 One notable counter-example to this is Brooks's novel *World War Z*, in which states attempt to implement the "Redeker Plan" in order to limit the zombie contagion. The plan begins with the recognition that it is impossible to save everyone, and therefore "safe zones" need to be established where military forces are consolidated and reinforced. A small percentage of citizens are then evacuated to the safe zone "not only to provide a labor pool for the eventual wartime economic restoration, but also to preserve the legitimacy and stability of the government, to prove to those already within the zone that their leaders were 'looking out for them.'" See Brooks, *World War Z*, 109. Importantly, the citizens left behind become "human bait" to distract the undead from following the retreat to the safe zone.
51 Thomas Hobbes and J. C. A. Gaskin, *Leviathan* (Oxford: Oxford University Press, 1998), i. xiii. 9.
52 Richard Matheson, *I Am Legend* (New York: Fawcett Publications, 1954).
53 Brooks, *World War Z*, 60.
54 David Wellington, *Monster Island, A Zombie Novel* (New York: Thunder's Mouth Press, 2006).
55 Manuel Loureiro, *Apocalypse Z: The Beginning of the End*, trans. Pamela Carmell (New York: AmazonCrossing, 2012).
56 In Stephen King's *Cell: A Novel* (New York: Scribner Publishing, 2006), technology is more directly the channel by which the "virus" spreads. Cell phone users are infected by a virus through their phones that turns them into zombie-like killers.
57 Brooks, *World War Z*, 338.
58 See Naim, "5 Wars of Globalization."
59 See, for example, Janice Thomson, *Mercenaries, Pirates, and Sovereigns: State-Building and Extraterritorial Violence in Early Modern Europe* (Princeton, NJ: Princeton University Press, 1994).
60 David Mizejewski, "Zombies vs. Animals? The Living Dead Wouldn't Stand a Chance," *Boing Boing*, October 14, 2013, http://boingboing.net/2013/10/14/zombiesvsanimals.html.
61 Skipp, *Zombies*, 698.

4
The Limits of Zombies: Monsters for a Neoliberal Age

David Schmid

Abstract: *This chapter asks what monsters most accurately represent in our current age of global neoliberalism. Although the ravenous hunger and destructiveness of zombies capture aspects of the brutal rapacity of contemporary capitalism, this chapter argues that many recent theoretical appropriations of the figure of the zombie are either opportunistic or overly simplistic in the way they use zombies as a symptom for the evils of the neoliberal world order. Moreover, the usefulness of the zombie as a way of analyzing the current conjuncture is limited by what this chapter calls the excessive visibility of this figure; the instantaneous visual impression made by the zombies that throng popular culture hides the fact that the true monsters of neoliberalism—psychopaths—hide in plain sight by means of their bland normality.*

Castillo, David R., David Schmid, David A. Reilly and John Edgar Browning. *Zombie Talk: Culture, History, Politics.* New York: Palgrave Macmillan, 2016.
DOI: 10.1057/9781137567727.0008.

The Limits of Zombies   93

When I began working on this chapter, my aim was to focus on the monster that best embodies and thematizes the ideological preoccupations, biases, and anxieties of the age of neoliberalism. My initial candidate was the zombie, especially the rapidly-moving zombies debuted in Danny Boyle's 2002 film *28 Days Later* and increasingly prevalent in popular culture thereafter. So, what happened to this plan? I began to read critical analyses of zombies and a variety of other monsters, the vast majority of which argued that these monsters were, in one way or another, symptoms of the cultures or the times that produced them (unlike Browning who, in his chapter, insinuates that the "symptom" is not the zombie, but rather how survival is negotiated). The more of these analyses I read, the more I was struck by the limitations of this symptomatic method of analyzing the meanings of monsters. Consequently, I decided to broaden the terms of the discussion beyond the zombie to the figure of the monster in general. To be precise, I want to use the limitations of symptomatic monsters to rethink the monstrous, to ask what it means from both a theoretical and a strategic viewpoint to use monstrosity both to read and critique neoliberalism.

The first step in this inquiry is to discuss whether the concept of the monstrous should be used in a predominantly negative or positive sense. As we know, the label of "monster" has been used in a multitude of historical, geographical, and ideological contexts to dismiss and demonize that which is considered marginal, deviant, and abject. But there have also been a number of attempts to resignify "monster" as a positive term in much the same way as gay, lesbian, bisexual, and transgendered activists, for example, have resignified the word "queer." Sometimes these attempts can be quite facile. In a 2009 article entitled "The Left and the Living Dead" journalist Paul Waldman argues that

> While one can certainly use zombies to express all kinds of ideas, I would argue that at heart, the genre is a progressive one.... A small group of people from varying backgrounds are thrust together and find that they can transcend their differences of age, race, and gender.... Surviving the tide of zombies requires community and mutual responsibility. What could be more progressive than that?[1]

It's not that such arguments are wrong necessarily (although most groups in zombie films do not behave in the way that Waldman describes—if they did, their survival rate would be much higher!); it's just that they leave so much out that one wonders whether the accuracy of their claims matters in any substantive sense.

DOI: 10.1057/9781137567727.0008

A more promising example of monstrous resignification is embodied in feminist theorist Donna Haraway's resonant phrase, "The Promises of Monsters." For Haraway, this promise is epitomized by the transgressive potential of the figure of the cyborg, which can perhaps challenge patriarchal, misogynist, and anthropocentric thought. In this reading, the monster's ability to confound categories, to trouble normally stable distinctions, and to blur boundaries that are otherwise clear is to be celebrated, and perhaps even harnessed as a revolutionary strategy. A more recent example of this kind of argument can be found in Michael Hardt and Antonio Negri's 2004 book *Multitude*, a necessarily plural concept that reminds us that what we're resignifying is not a singular entity but rather a series of images that have all, at different times, been seen by hegemonic social formations as examples of unruly, possibly dangerous power, such as the proletariat, the crowd, and the so-called "dangerous classes." According to Hardt and Negri, "What is so fearsome about the multitude is its indefinite number... it is composed of innumerable elements that remain different, one from the other, and yet communicate, collaborate, that act in common."[2] The fearsomeness of the multitude encourages Hardt and Negri to resignify monsters as embodying a liberatory potentiality. In their words, "the monsters begin to form new, alternative networks of affection and social organization.... We need to find the means to realize this monstrous power of the flesh of the multitude to form a new society."[3] Hardt and Negri conclude by saying that "The new world of monsters is where humanity has to grasp its future."[4]

There is much to recommend such positive resignifications of the meaning of monstrosity. They can act as a rallying cry for all those who feel themselves abjected by the current politico-economic order, giving them a way to make their exclusion both the point at which resistance begins and common cause with others who feel themselves to be left out. But even if we leave aside the question of how likely it is that such a multitudinous monstrous uprising will happen, there is still the issue of whether we should give up on "monster" as a pejorative term. Despite the fact that it seems old-fashioned, we should insist that neoliberalism is "monstrous" in the traditional sense, and that doing so is important both descriptively (i.e., in terms of accurately describing what neoliberalism is and what it does) and strategically (i.e., highlighting that the ethical and moral, as well as political and economic, monstrosity of neoliberalism is an important way to generate and focus public anger about its many depredations). In what follows, therefore, I will be using the concept of the monstrous predominantly, although not exclusively, in a negative sense, to refer both to damaging actions and ideologies and to a process that renders people and things abject.

With the tension between negative and positive readings of the monstrous in mind, I want to move on to an examination and critique of symptomatic readings of monsters. In its most general form, the monster as symptom appears as a way of focusing the zeitgeist of any given period, as in this passage from Jeffrey Jerome Cohen's preface to his important anthology *Monster Theory*: "fin de siècle America, a society that has created and commodified 'ambient fear'—a kind of total fear that saturates day-to-day living, prodding and silently antagonizing but never speaking its own name. This anxiety manifests itself symptomatically as a cultural fascination with monsters."[5] Not surprisingly, there has been a distinct upswing in both monster narratives and symptomatic readings of such narratives since 9/11, and many such readings have focused on the figure of the zombie in particular. In Kyle Bishop's 2009 article "Dead Man Still Walking: Explaining the Zombie Renaissance," he argues that

> Since the terrorist attacks of September 11, 2001, zombie movies have become more popular than ever, with multiple remakes, parodies, and sequels. This renaissance of the subgenre reveals a connection between zombie cinema and post-9/11 cultural consciousness. Horror films function as barometers of society's anxieties, and zombie movies represent the inescapable realities of unnatural death while presenting a grim view of the modern apocalypse through scenes of deserted streets, piles of corpses, and gangs of vigilantes.[6]

The zombie has actually had quite a long after-life in writing about monsters, not only in the post-9/11 context, but also before, as many commentators have described the zombie as an objective correlative for capitalism. In her 2006 book *Pretend We're Dead: Capitalist Monsters in American Pop Culture*, Annalee Newitz argues that

> One type of story that has haunted America since the late nineteenth century focuses on humans turned into monsters by capitalism. Mutated by backbreaking labor, driven insane by corporate conformity, or gorged on too many products of a money-hungry media industry, capitalism's monsters cannot tell the difference between commodities and people.... And because they spend so much time working, they often feel dead themselves.[7]

The virtues of such passages include reminding us that Karl Marx himself famously compares capital to a monster: "Capital is dead labour, that, vampire-like, only lives by sucking living labour, and lives the more, the more labour it sucks."[8]

My intent, in other words, is not to dismiss symptomatic readings of monstrosity out of hand. When Newitz goes on to argue that monster stories represent the subjective experience of alienation and that the "history of capitalism can be told as a monster story from beginning to end,"[9] I think she provides a useful way of thinking about the popularity of monster narratives. More specifically, I think work by critics such as Newitz can capture something of the savagery of capitalism in general and neoliberalism in particular.

This savagery comes across even more clearly in the recent work of Henry Giroux. In his 2011 book, *Zombie Politics and Culture in the Age of Casino Capitalism*, Giroux attempts, in his words,

> to develop a new form of political critique forged out of what may seem an extreme metaphor, the zombie or hyper-dead. Yet the metaphor is particularly apt for drawing attention to the ways in which political culture and power in American society now work in the interests of bare survival, if not disposability, for the vast majority of people.[10]

Although criticism of this kind sometimes seems to be proliferating faster than the zombies themselves, it can still contain useful observations, as when Chris Harman in his 2010 book *Zombie Capitalism* argues "that 21st century capitalism as a whole is a zombie system, seemingly dead when it comes to achieving human goals and responding to human feelings, but capable of sudden spurts of activity that cause chaos all around."[11]

So, critical work on culturally symptomatic monsters definitely has many strengths, but what are its weaknesses? For one, its use of monsters can be either opportunistic and/or lazy. For example, when one reads all of Harman's book, it's clear that the figure of the zombie is being used for its buzzword value as a hook to catch the reader rather than being the focus of the analysis in any substantive sense. Henry Giroux, for his part, tends to use "zombie" much too loosely, so that it describes not only the operations of predatory capitalists but also (as Giroux sees it) the mindlessness of popular culture and its consumers: "Instead of organized, massive protests against casino capitalism, the American public is treated to an endless and arrogant display of wealth, greed, and power. Armies of zombies tune in to gossip-laden entertainment, game, and reality TV shows, transfixed by the empty lure of celebrity culture."[12]

But there is a limitation to symptomatic readings of monsters much more profound than their use by political opportunists or their overly loose application, as Evan Calder Williams explains in his 2011 book *Combined and Uneven Apocalypse*:

> these readings about the "real" content of zombies are limited because they aren't really readings: they just describe what happens in the films. To say that the ending of *Night of the Living Dead*, with the "accidental" murder of an African-American man by the white redneck zombie hunting mob, is largely about race relations is just to say that you've watched the movie all the way through.[13]

Even if Williams is perhaps overly withering here, he does have a point. Symptomatic readings of monster narratives ironically all too often end up commenting only on the surface of such narratives, despite their pretension to depth. Symptomatic readings of monsters should be the starting point of critical inquiry, yet they are usually its conclusion.

Is such a problem or limitation inescapable? Ironically, despite his acerbic comments, Williams himself goes on to produce what can be described as a slightly more sophisticated symptomatic reading: "This is the particularity of what the figure of the zombie does and its position in the mass culture of capitalism. It thinks how real abstractions work on real bodies, of the nastiest intersections of the law of value and the law of inevitable decay."[14] Once again, the problem is not so much that such readings are inaccurate; it's that they are too easy, drawing a kind of one-to-one connection between cultural product and cultural context that oversimplifies the ways in which culture works and freezes the product into one kind of reading.

With this limitation in mind, we need to consider the possibility that traditional monsters, as tools of critique, are simply worn out and need to be rethought, as Williams argues:

> There is indeed something we have to kill now, as much as we can ever interfere in the unholy recombinatory mechanisms of advertising departments, massive cultural production, word of mouth, and various ways to make sexy zombie Halloween costumes. No more zombies, not now, not while the nightmare image of our times has become equally a dollar sign.[15]

While I agree with Williams that zombies need to be dispatched with efficient brutality from cultural critique (at least for the time being), I also want to insist that some concept of monstrosity is still necessary as a theoretical and strategic tool of critique. Why? At the most basic level, because I still believe in the well-known phrase attributed to Antonio

Gramsci: "The old world is dying away, and the new world struggles to come forth: now is the time of monsters."[16]

With the timeliness of monsters in mind, we need to find a different way to think about and use monsters in cultural criticism, and if we commit ourselves to that project, one problem we will need to grapple with is the excessive visibility of monsters, the way in which most monsters (zombies, vampires, werewolves, etc.) are immediately recognizable as such. Why is this a problem? Because visible monsters keep us locked into a structure of spectacle of the kind described by Alain Badiou in his 2010 book *The Communist Hypothesis*:

> The way the global financial crisis is described to us makes it look like one of those big bad films that are concocted by the ready-made hit machine that we now call the "cinema". It's all there: the gradual spectacle of the disaster, the crude manipulation of suspense...the terrifying repercussions...everything is collapsing, everything is going to collapse.[17]

Think of how little attention is paid to the cause of infection in such films as *28 Days Later* and *28 Weeks Later* because our attention is meant to be riveted on the spectacle of destruction and you can see what Badiou means.

The problem of visibility is compounded by the fact that the contemporary monsters of capitalism and neoliberalism are likely to be invisible, as Williams argues: "they constantly rear their figurative heads, yes. But because they are not accidents but necessary functions and consequences of the capitalist world system, they are structural blindspots."[18] The invisibility of the monsters characteristic of contemporary capitalism is an index of the fact that they are examples of what Slavoj Žižek in his 2008 book, *Violence: Six Sideways Reflections*, calls "objective violence," which he describes as "the often catastrophic consequences of the smooth functioning of our economic and political systems."[19] According to Žižek, objective violence is to be distinguished from its opposite, subjective violence, which he describes as "violence performed by a clearly identifiable agent."[20] Crucially, Žižek argues that a concentration on subjective violence represents a kind of trap for the spectator, in the sense that it makes it more difficult for us to perceive the objective violence that characterizes the everyday operating functions of capitalism: "The lesson is thus that one should resist the fascination of subjective violence, of violence enacted by social agents, evil individuals, disciplined repressive apparatuses, fanatical crowds."[21] Most of the violence enacted by monsters, including zombies, in our popular culture is "subjective violence" as defined by Žižek, and consequently focusing only on this violence makes it more difficult to see the violence of capitalism in general and neoliberalism in particular. This does not mean that we need to give up on monsters entirely, but it does mean that it might be more profitable to concentrate our attention on a particular type of monster: the psychopath, a category that includes not just celebrity serial killers and the larger-than-life homicidal protagonists of slasher movies (with whom the audience is meant to identify and even sympathize) but also the studiously anonymous, practically invisible CEO and politician. This is a figure with much greater potential to bring the monstrosity of neoliberalism into focus precisely because the psychopath blends invisibly into its background, being practically impossible to distinguish from "ordinary, normal" people.

Before going any further, however, I want to define exactly what I mean by neoliberalism. For the purposes of this essay, I follow the definition of neoliberalism offered by David Harvey. In its most neutral sense, Harvey describes neoliberalism in his 2005 book *A Brief History of Neoliberalism* as "a theory of political economic practices that proposes that human well-being can best be advanced by liberating individual entrepreneurial freedoms and skills within an institutional framework characterized by strong private property rights, free markets, and free trade."[22] Harvey goes on to make his definition more argumentative by emphasizing that capitalist liberalism freed of regulatory constraints is inevitably violent: "endless capital accumulation implies that the neoliberal regime of rights must be geographically expanded across the globe by violence...by imperialist practices (such as those of the World Trade Organization, the IMF and the World Bank) or through primitive accumulation."[23] And in his more recent book, 2010's *The Enigma of Capital*, Harvey makes clear that this violence derives in part from the fact that neoliberalism has a definite class character:

> it refers to a class project that coalesced in the crisis of the 1970s. Masked by a lot of rhetoric about individual freedom, liberty, personal responsibility and the virtues of privatization, the free market and free trade, it legitimized draconian policies designed to restore and consolidate capitalist class power. This project has been successful, judging by the incredible centralization of wealth and power observable in all those countries that took the neoliberal road. And there is no evidence that it is dead.[24]

Harvey's reference to death makes the temptation to refer to zombies at this point almost overwhelming, but I'm going to move them firmly to one side and instead bring the psychopath to the center of the stage.

What can a focus on the psychopath contribute to an understanding of the violence of neoliberalism? To answer that question, I first want to establish some of the basic definitional features of the psychopath. Psychopathy, like monstrosity, is a notoriously imprecise and flexible concept, but most commentators would agree that some combination of the following attributes make up a psychopathic personality: glibness and superficial charm; a grandiose sense of self-worth; a need for stimulation, combined with a proneness to boredom; pathological lying; a tendency to be cunning and manipulative; a lack of remorse or guilt; shallow affect; callousness and a lack of empathy; poor behavioral control; and a lack of willingness to accept responsibility for one's actions.

To make an obvious point, there is no shortage of psychopathic behavior among the rich and powerful. In an article entitled, "Schwarzenegger, DSK, and Gingrich: Do We Have Psychopaths Misruling Our World?" (from which I harvested my checklist of psychopathic traits), journalist Greg Guma analyzes the headline-making misadventures of actor and politician Arnold Schwarzenegger, former head of the IMF Dominique Strauss-Kahn, and US Republican politician Newt Gingrich and argues that "What the three men have in common, aside from wielding more influence than they can handle or deserve, is that their serial misbehavior went unchecked for years. In fact, it was rationalized as mere exuberance, frequently excused in "exceptional" people, when it actually demonstrated something else—ruling class impunity."[25] I have no problem with these men being called out for what may indeed be psychopathic behavior, especially if it succeeds in arousing populist anger against the rich and powerful. At the same time, however, it seems to me that such rabble-rousing is the least interesting way to apply the category of the psychopath to these figures. Why? The problem again is one of excessive visibility. If we confine our analysis only to those members of the power elite that make it into the headlines, we risk focusing only on representative or symptomatic individuals, rather than developing a properly institutional and structural reading of monstrosity.

That's not to say that critique should not focus on individuals at all; indeed, there is a disturbing trend in some leftist work on corporations that arguably lets corporate executives off the hook by presenting them as caught up in a system where they *have* to make psychopathic decisions. According to this view, executives can only protect themselves from this fact by schizophrenically compartmentalizing their lives, thus making the executives sound like the victims of the corporations for which they work, corporations that are then portrayed by these same analyses as unambiguously monstrous. Although the people Hardt and Negri have described as "the leaders of major corporations...the political leaders of dominant nation-states and the bureaucrats of the supranational economic institutions"[26] do not necessarily conspire together as a class, they do, as Harvey puts it,

> nevertheless possess a certain accordance of interests that generally recognizes the advantages...to be derived from neoliberalization. They also possess, through organizations like the World Economic Forum in Davos, means of exchanging ideas and of consorting and consulting with political leaders. They exercise immense influence over global affairs and possess a freedom of action that no ordinary citizen possesses.[27]

Given these facts, it is appropriate that these people be both the focus of critique and held to account, something that hardly ever happens.

With this said, it is all too easy to go from the extreme of seeing the power elite as essentially innocent to the opposite extreme, a monstrous cabal in complete charge of the world order. Although it sounds like a strange claim, Williams has argued that it's too tempting to create an account where these people are in charge. In the context of discussing John Carpenter's 1988 sci-fi film *They Live*, Williams states that

> The film is not really the allegory of the "alienated" injustice of capitalism it plays at being. It is the wish-image of an absent clarity, and it is the necessary frustration of such desire. For lingering behind the sense that, can you imagine how awful it would be if the world was run by powerful aliens?, is the real question: wouldn't it be nice if it were run by powerful aliens, if we could find some inhuman driver at the wheel, if we knew who to blame all along? Isn't that what we really want, to know once and for all that there is some conspiratorial reason and order behind the blind contingencies of the world order?[28]

To resist this deeply satisfying but counter-productive simplicity, we need to apply the interpretive lens of psychopathy not only to the members of the power elite but also to the structures and institutions they inhabit.

An article by journalist Johann Hari on the Dominique Strauss-Kahn affair illustrates this necessity powerfully. According to Hari,

> the fact that Dominique Strauss-Kahn, the former head of the International Monetary Fund (IMF), is facing trial for allegedly raping a maid in a New York hotel room is—rightly—big news. But imagine a prominent figure was

charged not with raping a maid, but starving her to death, along with her children, her parents, and thousands of other people. That is what the IMF has done to innocent people in the recent past. That is what it will do again, unless we transform it beyond all recognition.[29]

Hari illustrates his claim about the IMF by concentrating on the example of the southeast African country of Malawi (although this example could be replicated many times over in other parts of the world).

In the 1990s, Malawi was experiencing economic problems so severe that they had to ask the IMF for help. The "help" that the IMF provided was conditional upon Malawi submitting to a structural adjustment program, which involved privatizing state-run industries, cutting state spending on the poor, and selling off stockpiles of grain to pay international bankers the interest on the loans they had given Malawi. When the crops failed, Malawi experienced the worst famine in its history because the government had almost no resources to hand out to its starving population. In the middle of the famine, in which at least a thousand people died, the IMF withheld $47 million dollars in aid because it was displeased by what it saw as the slow pace at which Malawi's government was implementing market reforms. The aid organization ActionAid subsequently conducted an investigation into the famine. They concluded that the IMF bears responsibility for the disaster.

What happened in Malawi is a classic example of neoliberalism at work. The country was systematically made over into what Harvey calls a "neoliberal state," which he defines as being characterized by "a state apparatus whose fundamental mission was to facilitate conditions for profitable capital accumulation on the part of both domestic and foreign capital."[30] This is the process that leads Hari to conclude that

> It is not only Strauss-Kahn who should be on trial. It is the institution he has been running...if we took the idea of human equality seriously, and remembered all the people who have been impoverished, starved and killed by this institution, we would be discussing the establishment of a Truth and Reconciliation Commission—and how to disband the IMF entirely and start again.[31]

Because, as Harvey puts it, neoliberalism is designed to "reflect the interests of private property owners, businesses, multinational corporations, and financial capital,"[32] we must also include the corporation in our inquiry and see whether the category of the psychopath sheds light on the purpose and functioning of that organization. There is a long history of the corporation being seen as a monstrous entity. To take just one example, US Supreme Court Justice Louis Brandeis, dissenting from a Supreme Court decision in 1933, argued that "coincident with the growth of these giant corporations, there has occurred a marked concentration of individual wealth; and...the resulting disparity in incomes is a major cause of the existing depression. Such is the Frankenstein monster which states have created by their corporation laws."[33]

This view of the corporation as monstrous animates the work of a journal like *Multinational Monitor*, which was founded by consumer advocate Ralph Nader in 1980, and which focuses on labor issues, occupational safety and health, the environment, globalization, privatization, and developing nations. Every year, the magazine publishes a list of "The Top Ten Worst Corporations," which names the worst offenders in the areas of "corporate crime, negligence and dastardly behavior." Companies that made the list in recent years include BP, Delphi, DuPont, ExxonMobil, Ford, Halliburton, KPMG, Roche, BAE, Boeing, FirstEnergy, Pfizer, and Wal-Mart. The *Multinational Monitor* is also well-known for its "Lawrence Summers Memorial Award," an award given each issue in satirical honor of Lawrence Summers, the Secretary of the Treasury under Bill Clinton, later President of Harvard University, and most recently Director of the White House National Economic Council for Barack Obama, given to companies that "take extraordinary leaps to justify unethical practices." The award refers to the infamous memo written by Summers' aide Lant Pritchett in 1991, when Summers was the World Bank's Chief Economist. The memo advocated transferring toxic waste and pollution from developed countries to the least developed countries. (Summers later stated the memo was meant to be satirical.)

The argument that the corporation is specifically psychopathic rather than generally monstrous is of more recent vintage and is exemplified by Joel Bakan's 2004 book, *The Corporation: The Pathological Pursuit of Profit and Power*. Bakan argues that "The corporation's legally defined mandate is to pursue, relentlessly and without exception, its own self-interest, regardless of the often harmful consequences it might cause to others. As a result...the corporation is a pathological institution, a dangerous possessor of the great power it wields over people and societies."[34] Consequently, according to Bakan, the harm that corporations do to others is regarded neutrally as the inevitable consequence of economic activity—people hurt are regarded as nothing more than "externalities."

Although I do not have the space in this chapter to offer readings of films or written texts to substantiate this view of the capitalist and the corporation as the monsters of neoliberalism, if I were to do so, I would concentrate not on zombie or vampire movies, but on such films as Charles Ferguson's 2010 documentary *Inside Job*, which examines the financial crisis of 2007–10, and which Ferguson has described as being about "the systemic corruption of the United States by the financial services industry and the consequences of that systemic corruption."[35] And if I were looking for a suitably monstrous environment to explore, I wouldn't choose a zombie's grave or a vampire's castle, but Ciudad Juarez, the epicenter of Mexico's ongoing drug war and one of the most violent cities in the world. In a recent article, journalist Ed Vulliamy has argued that "Narco-cartels are not pastiches of global corporations, nor are they errant bastards of the global economy—they are pioneers of it. They point, in their business logic and modus operandi, to how the legal economy will arrange itself next."[36] Consequently, Vulliamy goes on to argue, and with Ciudad Juarez in mind,

> Mexico's war is how the future will look, because it belongs not in the 19th century with wars of empire, or the 20th with wars of ideology, race and religion—but utterly in a present to which the global economy is committed, and to a zeitgeist of frenzied materialism we adamantly refuse to temper: it is the inevitable war of capitalism gone mad.[37]

Bakan concludes *The Corporation* by making a number of recommendations about how the pernicious power and influence of corporations could be changed, including improving the regulatory system, strengthening political democracy, creating a robust public sphere, and challenging neoliberalism. "Nations," he says, "should work together to shift the ideologies and practices of international institutions, such as the WTO, IMF, and World Bank, away from market fundamentalism and its facilitation of deregulation and privatization."[38] I believe that the figure of the psychopath is one way in which a monster-focused critique can contribute to the changes that Bakan recommends, but I would like to conclude this essay by arguing that if we want to maximize the potential of a monstrous critique of neoliberalism, it might ultimately be more helpful to think of the monstrous as a *process* rather than a figure of any kind, be it zombie, vampire, psychopathic CEO, or financial institution. In other words, although monstrosity undoubtedly resides in a bewildering array of figures all of whom are symptomatic, in one way or another, of their respective political and cultural contexts, if we are to keep up with the flexibility and pace of neoliberal exploitation, we need to conceive of monstrosity not only as a symptom but also as a highly mobile, endlessly mutating, and extremely specific set of discourses, technologies, and ideologies, able to both adjust to local circumstances with great rapidity and abject (that is, render monstrous) anyone and anything that forms a barrier to capital accumulation. To counter this threat, our conception of the monstrous must be just as mobile and flexible.

With Vulliamy's pessimistic assessment of Ciudad Juarez in mind, one ray of hope can be found in the work of Mexico's Zapatista National Liberation Army, as described by Harvey in *The Enigma of Capital*:

> The Zapatista rebels...did not seek to take over state power or accomplish a political revolution. They sought instead to work through the whole of civil society in a more open and fluid search for alternatives that would look to answer to their specific needs as a cultural formation and to restore their own sense of dignity and respect.[39]

What Harvey is describing here is a different kind of revolution, one that works on a variety of spatial scales simultaneously, one that is extremely attentive to local conditions and the needs of people on the ground, and one that is highly mobile and flexible. These are all necessary features of thinking of the monstrous as a process.

After all, one of the most commonly misunderstood features of capital is the fact of its fluidity and flexibility. As Harvey puts it, "Capital is not a thing but a process in which money is perpetually sent in search of more money."[40] More to the point, it is the mobility of capital that makes it so destructive. According to Harman, it is capitalism's imperative toward constant motion that "creates periodic havoc for all those who live within it, a horrific hybrid of Frankenstein's monster and of Dracula, a human creation that has escaped control and lives by devouring the lifeblood of its creators."[41]

It may be too much to hope that we can regain control of the monster of neoliberalism, but we can at least develop the tools of critique that allow us to accurately recognize, diagnose, and challenge this highly mobile monster wherever it appears. In doing so, perhaps we will ultimately be able to redirect our attention to where, according to Badiou, it should be directed: "We will contrast the wicked spectacle of capitalism with the real of peoples, with the lives of people and the movement of ideas."[42] Can zombies play a role in achieving the aim that Badiou describes? Despite the skepticism I have expressed in this essay about the political efficacy of the zombie as a means of critiquing the excesses of neoliberalism, it is important to acknowledge the fact that this figure is going to remain a fixture in contemporary American culture for the foreseeable future. In this respect, the zombie remains filled with potential; in particular, it is entirely possible that the zombie can be turned into a shuffling, decaying, and moaning *lingua franca* by means of which critics can use the threat of apocalypse to help us all imagine what so often seems to be unimaginable: a future.

Notes

1. Paul Waldman, "The Left and the Living Dead: In the Event of a Zombie Apocalypse, Will Progressive Ideals Win Out?" *The American Prospect*, June 16, 2009, http://prospect.org/article/left-and-living-dead.
2. Michael Hardt and Antonio Negri, *Multitude: War and Democracy in the Age of Empire* (New York: Penguin Books, 2004), 140.
3. Ibid., 193.
4. Ibid., 196.
5. Jeffrey Jerome Cohen, "Preface: In a Time of Monsters," in *Monster Theory: Reading Culture*, ed. Jeffrey Jerome Cohen (Minneapolis: University of Minnesota Press, 1996), viii.
6. Kyle Bishop, "Dead Man Still Walking: Explaining the Zombie Renaissance," *Journal of Popular Film and Television* 37, no. 1 (2009): 17.
7. Annalee Newitz, *Pretend We're Dead: Capitalist Monsters in American Pop Culture* (Durham, NC: Duke University Press, 2006), 2.
8. Karl Marx, "Chapter Ten: The Working-Day," in *Capital, Volume One*, *Marxists Internet Archive*. Accessed June 2, 2015. https://www.marxists.org/archive/marx/works/1867-c1/ch10.htm.
9. Newitz, *Pretend We're Dead*, 6, 12.
10. Henry A. Giroux, *Zombie Politics and Culture in the Age of Casino Capitalism* (New York: Peter Lang, 2011), 23.
11. Chris Harman, *Zombie Capitalism: Global Crisis and the Relevance of Marx* (Chicago: Haymarket Books, 2010), 12.
12. Giroux, *Zombie Politics and Culture in the Age of Casino Capitalism*, 4.
13. Evan Calder Williams, *Combined and Uneven Apocalypse* (Winchester, UK: Zero Books, 2011), 78.
14. Ibid., 80.
15. Ibid., 143.
16. Quoted in Slavoj Žižek, *Living in the End Times* (New York: Verso, 2011), 479.

17 Alain Badiou, *The Communist Hypothesis* (New York: Verso Books, 2010), 91.
18 Williams, *Combined and Uneven Apocalypse*, 150.
19 Slavoj Žižek, *Violence: Six Sideways Reflections* (London: Profile Books, 2008), 1.
20 Ibid.
21 Ibid., 10.
22 David Harvey, *A Brief History of Neoliberalism* (New York: Oxford University Press, 2005), 2.
23 Ibid., 181–2.
24 David Harvey, *The Enigma of Capital* (New York: Oxford University Press, 2010), 10.
25 Greg Guma, "Schwarzenegger, DSK, and Gingrich: Do We Have Psychopaths Misruling Our World?" *Alternet*, May 19, 2011, http://www.alternet.org/story/151014/schwarzenegger,_dsk,_and_gingrich%3A_do_we_have_psychopaths_misruling_our_world.
26 Hardt and Negri, *Multitude*, 167.
27 Harvey, *A Brief History of Neoliberalism*, 36.
28 Williams, *Combined and Uneven Apocalypse*, 7.
29 Johann Hari, "It's Not Just Dominique Strauss-Kahn. The IMF Itself Should Be on Trial," *The Independent*, June 3, 2011, http://www.independent.co.uk/voices/commentators/johann-hari/johann-hari-its-not-just-dominique-strausskahn-the-imf-itself-should-be-on-trial-2292270.html.
30 Harvey, *A Brief History of Neoliberalism*, 7.
31 Hari, "It's Not Just Dominique Strauss-Kahn."
32 Harvey, *A Brief History of Neoliberalism*, 7.
33 Louis Brandeis, "Louis K. Liggett Co. v. Lee, 288 U.S. 517 (1933)," *FindLaw.com*, accessed August 2, 2012, http://caselaw.findlaw.com/us-supreme-court/288/517.html.
34 Joel Bakan, *The Corporation: The Pathological Pursuit of Profit and Power* (New York: Free Press, 2004), 1–2.
35 Charles Ferguson, dir., *Inside Job* (Hollywood, Los Angeles, CA: Sony Pictures Classics, 2010), DVD.
36 Ed Vulliamy, "The Drug War Is the Inevitable Result of Capitalism Gone Mad; Ciudad Juarez is All of Our Futures," *Alternet*, June 21, 2011, http://www.alternet.org/story/151361/the_drug_war_is_the_inevitable_result_of_capitalism_gone_mad%3B_ciudad_juarez_is_all_of_our_futures.
37 Ibid.
38 Bakan, *The Corporation*, 164.
39 Harvey, *The Enigma of Capital*, 252.
40 Ibid., 40.
41 Harman, *Zombie Capitalism*, 85.
42 Badiou, *The Communist Hypothesis*, 100.

Afterword: What Are We Talking About When We Talk About Zombies?

William Egginton

Abstract: *This afterword argues that what unifies as well as distinguishes this volume from the many analyses that have preceded it is the combination of a historical materialist approach to explaining the popularity of the undead with an unusual openness to questioning the underlying assumptions and efficacy of such explanations. In other words, the authors assembled here manage both to ask what zombies mean in late capitalist society and what it can possibly mean for zombies to mean something.*

Castillo, David R., David Schmid, David A. Reilly and John Edgar Browning. *Zombie Talk: Culture, History, Politics*. New York: Palgrave Macmillan, 2016. DOI: 10.1057/9781137567727.0009.

A specter is haunting the academy—the specter of the undead.

Such could be an appropriate opening for the afterword to a volume that focuses the beam of Marxist-inflected critical theory on the mass-cultural phenomenon of zombies. And what a phenomenon they have become. As the contributors to this volume note, zombies—the rambling, post-apocalyptic, multitudinous variety as opposed to the voodoo-induced loners of Caribbean lore—have spread like a virulent contagion since their introduction in George A. Romero's 1968 *Night of the Living Dead*, itself an adaptation of the novel from 14 years earlier *I Am Legend* (as John Edgar Browning details in the first chapter). Indeed, my own quick survey on the Google Ngram Viewer shows a steep incline in English-language mentions starting in the year that seminal gorefest was released, amounting to a more than 1,000% increase in the appearance of zombies in print by 2008, the last year surveyed.

The four scholars whose pieces form this study are far from the first to analyze this pop-culture explosion; and they will certainly not be the last. What unifies as well as distinguishes this volume from the many analyses that have preceded it, however, is the combination of a historical materialist approach to explaining the popularity of the undead with an unusual openness to questioning the underlying assumptions and efficacy of such explanations. In other words, the authors assembled here manage both to ask what zombies mean in late capitalist society *and* what it can possibly mean for zombies to mean something.

In the volume's last contribution, David Schmid draws attention to the limitations of "symptomatic readings" of zombies in popular culture, which depend on claims such as Kyle Bishop's that, "[h]orror films function as barometers of society's anxieties, and zombie movies represent the inescapable realities of unnatural death while presenting a grim view of the modern apocalypse through scenes of deserted streets, piles of corpses, and gangs of vigilantes."[1]

For Schmid, while monsters in general and zombies in particular can be read metaphorically as reminders of the monstrous aspects of neoliberalism, the concomitant risk such readings carry with them is that the very same monsters, in the "excessive visibility" of the "subjective violence" that they commit and that is committed against them, can blind us to the very real "objective violence" of a neoliberal political economy whose devastation continues unabated. As a critical antidote to this visibility, he proposes the psychopath as a perhaps more apt monster for the age of neoliberal domination, borrowing from Joel Bakan's 2004 argument that the corporation, whose "legally defined mandate is to pursue, relentlessly and without exception, its own self-interest, regardless of the often harmful consequences it might cause to others,"[2] is nothing other than a legally sanctioned psychopath, and in fact one on which the entire neoliberal order is founded.

Yet while zombies commit subjective violence in excessively visible ways on our screens, critically informed attention to their role on those screens and the appeal they generate need not be distracted by that visibility from the hidden but almost universal violence that is, using T. S. Eliot's term, their objective correlative. In other words, would not a symptomatic reading attuned to such objective violence give us clues as to how the undeniable *appeal* of zombies overlays or responds to an implicit knowledge on the part of the consumers of that hidden violence, and how the cloistered, suburban lives of late capitalist consumers rest uneasily over the shallow grave of abject multitudes? Such a reading would need to explain the very mechanism of that appeal, the reason why the consumer class of the culture industry would on the one hand seek to erase the suffering legions produced by an economy of extraction while on the other greedily devouring their avatars in fictional form.

One such mechanism could be the psychoanalytic notion of fantasy, advanced most explicitly in this volume by David R. Castillo. Comparing some modern horror stories with their early modern precedents, he argues that "the revelations and warnings that come with our dark fantasies are both enduring and historically specific. Thus, death (to provide a particularly apt example) may well be a trans-historical source of anxiety, but our dark fantasies reflect/reshape our anxiety about death in historically specific modes." That our "dark fantasies" somehow reflect or reshape our anxieties is a classic psychoanalytic assertion, which Castillo embraces, along with feminist and socio-political methodologies, as being necessary for understanding the appeal of "our favorite monsters." The anxieties he locates at the core of our fantasies about zombies are precisely anxieties provoked by the late capitalist mode of production and its effects.

David A. Reilly agrees and expands on such an explanation in his contribution, arguing that, among the spectrum of defensible "meanings" that zombies carry—from the communist threat to fear of contagions like AIDS to simply an excuse for vicarious gratuitous slaughter—the most promising stems from our gradual confrontation with apocalyptic globalization, the knowledge that "we are on a trajectory that is unsustainable, and that may have devastating global consequences." Reilly further connects this knowledge to the expansion of information technology, arguing that "we suffer from *information glut*: a paralyzing overabundance of information that requires expertise to wade through and to interpret."

This information glut maps directly onto the seemingly inevitable trend of globalized capitalism to concentrate ever-greater wealth in the hands of the few by extracting ever more resources from the many, leaving vast portions of the world's population underemployed or exploited and, in some cases, not even fit for exploitation—in Niklas Luhmann's famous words, "there is nothing to exploit in the favelas."[3] In other words, as producers proudly turn to new technologies (including and even especially information technologies) to obviate the need for employees, those of us still employed happily purchase their products, thereby contributing to the very economy that, according to Martin Ford's analysis in *Rise of the Robots: Technology and the Threat of a Jobless Future*, will inevitably drive us to obsolescence as well.[4]

Reilly sees in the zombie paradigm not only a metaphor for this apocalyptic scenario, but also a reason for its appeal: namely, the fantasy of a newly exerted autonomy. The zombie paradigm combines for viewers an Armageddon we know is coming with the fantasy of humanity unleashed from the bonds of governments and multinational corporations. The survivors who band together face mortal terror, but they are also "empowered to determine [their] own futures." This appeal corresponds, according to a psychoanalytic understanding of the appeal of horror in general, to the pleasure derived from the repetition of ostensibly negative scenarios—which Freud at one point hypothesized as a manner of attempting to master what exceeds our control—but it finds an almost exact analogue in Kant's theory of the sublime:

> The astonishment bordering on terror, the horror and the awesome shudder, which grip the spectator in viewing mountain ranges towering to the heavens, deep ravines and the raging torrents in them, deeply shadowed wastelands inducing melancholy reflection, etc., is, in view of the safety in which he knows himself to be, not actual fear, but only an attempt to involve ourselves in it by means of the imagination, in order to feel the power of that very faculty, to combine the movement of the mind thereby aroused with its calmness, and so to be superior to nature within us, and thus also that outside us, insofar as it can have an influence on our feeling of well-being.[5]

Indeed, Browning's contribution focuses on the structure and historical emergence of what he calls the "survival space" of zombie literature and movies, wherein the non-zombies gather to defend themselves against the swarming undead: "the cramming of a few disparate individuals into an enclosure or space and forcing them to work together in order to survive (or get killed if they do not) [was] a formula responsible for keeping the zombie pictures fresh, interesting, and relevant for over 45 years." Browning finds the origin of this essential structure in Richard Matheson's 1954 novel *I Am Legend*, which he also credits with having given rise to the multitudinous, swarming behavior of those zombies that—like almost all since then—do not owe their existence to a voodoo master.

Like Kant's spectator, these contributions imply that we enjoy watching the spectacle of our world's immolation in a zombie apocalypse in part because, from the safety in which we know ourselves to be relative to the events on the screen, we can activate the power of the imagination, which is simultaneously "a power to assert our independence in the face of the influences of nature." In activating that power and enjoying that sensation, we are simultaneously inserting ourselves into a fantasy of power and autonomy that staves off, for a time, the impending sense of a disaster to come.

The sign that a group of essays truly coheres is when, taken together, they yield a lesson larger than any one contribution. In fact it seems that the concert of these four voices has produced just such an insight, for by combining the question of the appeal of a particular monster in literature and film with that of the nature of symptomatic readings in general, the volume has ventured a new thought: that the appeal of this cultural figure may depend precisely on its problematic status as symptom. In other words, it is exactly because zombies stand in such conflicted relation to the socio-historical reality they emerge from that they exert such a fascination on their consumers.

This paradox is what lies at the heart of a cultural symptom, and what gives it its force. The symptom represents the socio-historical reality at the same time as it articulates an unconscious knowledge and a concomitant desire. That knowledge is simply that we are the agents of our own demise; like the slave Lacan writes of bearing the order for his own execution tattooed to his scalp,[6] our destruction is ensured by the very fulfillment of our functioning as autonomous consumers in a late capitalist economy. Zombies literalize that image in their relentless and cannibalistic drive to consume the human survivors; at the same time, the cells of human survivors evince the desire imbricated with that knowledge, a desire for freedom and self-determination from the economic forces that situate us as the agents of our own destruction.

This hinge between appeal and social reality is reinforced by yet another condensation: that between communication and production. As I noted above in reference to Reilly's argument, the "information glut" whereby today's consumers are overwhelmed by information about the world is superimposed on a kind of production glut, such that our urge to consume the latest technology becomes the mechanism whereby that same technology will gradually, inevitably eradicate the possibility of gainful employment for larger and larger sectors of the world's population. This is happening now because, as Castillo and I argue elsewhere,[7] we are living in an age of inflationary media. Unlike other times when there could be more truth to the vulgar Marxist notion that the means of production ultimately determine the content of culture, under the conditions of inflationary media, the means of production and the means of communication become conflated. To put it in simpler terms: the means become the media.

Whereas the mode of the capitalist is always to attempt to monopolize the means of production, in inflationary ages, that domination is explicitly over the media. Ownership of the media is concentrated in such a way that greater and greater portions of the population are exposed to messaging issued from smaller and smaller circles of influence. While it may seem that this generalization is counter to the proliferation of content providers on the web and cable outlets today, we need to see that this apparent diversity masks a profound trend toward the concentration and ownership of the media into fewer and ever more powerful hands. This oligarchy then brazenly uses its financial power to ensure unfettered influence over political processes in order to enable the continued exertion of its economic expansion.

In some ways, then, the ultimate zombie move of the twenty-first century was a millennial release that technically had no zombies in it. Nevertheless, the fantasy scenario painted by the 1999 film *The Matrix* firmly encapsulates the paradoxes and appeal of our fascination with the undead. For can it not be said that, in light of the arguments presented in this volume, we, the citizens of the early twenty-first century industrialized world, are like so many coppertop batteries, our brains plugged into a virtual world in which we live, play, and dream, while our bodies, i.e., our economic livelihood, are kept on life-support to be drained dry in the service of that economy? Everything is constructed so that we avert our gaze from this reality. We become zombie consumers of media—zombies because we are animate without anima, we believe we are alive, real, autonomous, but in reality we are already dead, plugged into the relentless machine of capital hell-bent on our destruction.

Maybe that's the real meaning of undead—already dead, but just alive enough not to realize it.

Notes

1. Kyle Bishop, "Dead Man *Still* Walking: Explaining the Zombie Renaissance," *Journal of Popular Film & Television* 37, no. 1 (2009): 17.
2. Joel Bakan, *The Corporation: The Pathological Pursuit of Profit and Power* (New York: Free Press, 2004), 1.
3. Niklas Luhmann, "Globalization or World Society? How to Conceive of Modern Society," *International Review of Sociology* 7, no. 1 (1997): 67.
4. Martin Ford, *Rise of the Robots: Technology and the Threat of a Jobless Future* (New York: Basic Books, 2015).
5. Immanuel Kant, *Critique of the Power of Judgment*, ed. Paul Guyer, trans. Paul Guyer and Eric Matthews (Cambridge: Cambridge University Press, 2000), 152.
6. Jacques Lacan, *Ecrits*, trans. Bruce Fink (New York: Norton, 2002), 671–702.
7. David Castillo and William Egginton, "The Architecture of Mourning," *Feedback*, September 12, 2014, http://openhumanitiespress.org/feedback/theory/the-architecture-of-mourning/.

Bibliography

28 Days Later. Directed by Danny Boyle. Los Angeles: Fox Searchlight Pictures, 2002.
28 Weeks Later. Directed by Juan Carlos Fresnadillo. Los Angeles: 20th Century Fox, 2007.
Abraham Lincoln Vampire Hunter. Directed by Timur Beckmambetov. Los Angeles: 20th Century Fox, 2012.
Adams, John, ed. *The Living Dead*. San Francisco: Night Shade Books, 2008.
Adkins, Brent. *Death and Desire in Hegel, Heidegger, and Deleuze*. Edinburgh: Edinburgh University Press, 2007.
Alley, Dodd. *Gamers and Gorehounds—The Influence of Video Games on the American Contemporary Horror Film*. Saarbrücken, Germany: Verlag Dr Müller Aktiengesellschaft & Co., 2007.
Arata, Stephen. "The Occidental Tourist: Dracula and the Anxiety of Reverse Colonization." In *The Horror Reader*, edited by Ken Gelder. New York: Routledge, 2000.
Badiou, Alain. *The Communist Hypothesis*. NY: Verso Books, 2010. Print.
Bakan, Joel. *The Corporation: The Pathological Pursuit of Profit and Power*. New York: Free Press, 2004.
Barber, Benjamin. *Jihad vs. McWorld: Terrorism's Challenge to Democracy*. New York: Ballantine Books, 1995.
Barber, Benjamin R. "Jihad vs. McWorld." *The Atlantic*, March 1992. http://www.theatlantic.com/magazine/archive/1992/03/jihad-vs-mcworld/303882/
Barber, Paul. *Vampires, Burial, and Death: Folklore and Reality*, New Haven, CT: Yale University Press, 1988.

Becker, Ernest. "A Note on Freud's Primal Horde Theory." *Psychoanalytic Quarterly* 30 (1961): 413–19.

Benedict, Barbara. *A Cultural History of Early Modern Inquiry.* Chicago: University of Chicago Press, 2001.

Berenstein, R. J. *Attack of the Leading Ladies: Gender, Sexuality, and Spectatorship in Classic Horror Cinema.* New York: Columbia University Press, 1996.

Birch-Bayley, Nicole. "Terror in Horror Genres: The Global Media and the Millennial Zombie." *The Journal of Popular Culture* 45, no. 6 (2012): 1137–51.

Bishop, Kyle. *American Zombie Gothic: The Rise and Fall (and Rise) of the Walking Dead in Popular Culture.* Jefferson, NC: McFarland and Company, 2010.

———. "Dead Man *Still* Walking: Explaining the Zombie Renaissance." *Journal of Popular Film and Television* 37, no. 1 (2009): 16–25.

The Birds. Directed by Alfred Hitchcock. Universal City, CA: Universal Pictures, 1963.

Blaut, J. M. *The Colonizer's Model of the World: Geographical Diffusionism and Eurocentric History.* New York: Guilford Press, 1993.

Booker, M. Keith. *Monsters, Mushroom Clouds, and the Cold War: American Science Fiction and the Roots of Postmodernism, 1946-1964.* Westport, CT: Greenwood Press, 2001.

Brandeis, Louis. "Louis K. Liggett Co. v. Lee, 288 U.S. 517 (1933)." *FindLaw.com.* Accessed August 2, 2012. http://caselaw.findlaw.com/us-supreme-court/288/517.html.

Brooks, Max. *World War Z: An Oral History of the Zombie War.* New York: Crown, 2006.

———. *The Zombie Survival Guide: Complete Protection from the Living Dead.* New York: Three Rivers Press, 2003.

Brown, Lawrence A. *Innovation Diffusion: A New Perspective.* New York: Methuen Press, 1981.

Buffy the Vampire Slayer. Directed by Joss Whedon. Los Angeles: 20th Television, 1997.

The Cabinet of Dr. Caligari. Directed by Robert Wiene. Berlin: Decla-Bioscop, 1920.

Carr, Nicholas. *The Glass Cage: Automation and Us.* New York: W. W. Norton & Company, 2014.

Carroll, Noël. "The Nature of Horror." *The Journal of Art Aesthetics and Art Criticism* 46, no. 1 (1987): 51–9.

———. *The Philosophy of Horror: Or, Paradoxes of the Heart*. New York: Routledge, 1990.

Castillo, David R. *(A)Wry Views: Anamorphosis, Cervantes and the Early Picaresque*. West Lafayette, IN: Purdue University Press, 2001.

———. *Baroque Horrors: Roots of the Fantastic in the Age of Curiosities*. Ann Arbor, MI: The University of Michigan Press, 2010.

Castillo, David and William Egginton. "The Architecture of Mourning." *Feedback*, September 12, 2014. http://openhumanitiespress.org/feedback/theory/the-architecture-of-mourning/.

Christie, Deborah and Sarah Juliet Lauro. *Better Off Dead: The Evolution of the Zombie as Post-Human*. New York: Fordham University Press, 2011.

Cohen, Jeffrey Jerome. "Preface: In a Time of Monsters." In *Monster Theory: Reading Culture*, edited by Jeffrey Jerome Cohen. Minneapolis: University of Minnesota Press, 1996.

Collins, Suzanne. *The Hunger Games*. New York: Scholastic Inc., 2008.

Conde, Víctor. *Naturaleza muerta*. Palma de Mallorca: Dolmen, 2009.

Conrad, Joseph. "Turgenev." In *Notes on Life and Letters*. Garden City, NY: Double, Page & Company, 1921.

Creed, Barbara. *The Monstrous-Feminine: Film, Feminism, Psychoanalysis*. New York: Routledge, 1993.

Daston, Lorraine and Katherine Park. *Wonders and the Order of Nature, 1150–1750*. New York: Zone Books, 1998.

Dawn of the Dead. Directed by George A. Romero. Beverly Hills, CA: United Film Distribution Company, 1978.

Dawn of the Dead. Directed by Zack Snyder. Universal City, CA: Universal Studios, 2004.

Day of the Dead. Directed by George A. Romero. Beverly Hills, CA: United Film Distribution Company, 1985.

Deleuze, Gilles, and Guattari, Felix. 1972. *Anti-Oedipus: Capitalism and Schizophrenia*, Minneapolis: University of Minnesota Press, 2000.

———. *A Thousand Plateaus: Capitalism and Schizophrenia*, Minneapolis: University of Minnesota Press, 1987.

Del Río Parra, Elena. *Una era de monstruos: Representaciones de lo deforme en el Siglo de Oro español*. Madrid: Iberoamericana, 2003.

Del Toro, Guillermo and Chuck Hogan. *The Night Eternal*. New York: HaperCollins Publishing, 2011.

Dennett, Daniel C. *Consciousness Explained*. New York: Little, Brown and Co., 1991.

de Tormes, Lázaro González-Pérez. *Lazarillo Z: Matar Zombies nunca fue pan comido*. Barcelona: Debolsillo, 2010.

Diary of the Dead. Directed by George A. Romero. New York: The Weinstein Company, 2007.

Dietle, David. "7 Scientific Reasons a Zombie Outbreak Would Fail (Quickly)." *Cracked*, August 17, 2010. http://www.cracked.com/article_18683_7-scientific-reasons-zombie-outbreak-would-fail-quickly.html#ixzz2yIoOFiyO.

Doc of the Dead. Directed by Alexandre O. Philippe. Denver, CO: Exhibit A Pictures, 2014.

Doomsday. Directed by Neil Marshall. Universal City, CA: Universal Pictures, 2008.

Falconer, Robert. "He Is Legend." *CinemaSpy.com*. Accessed December 11, 2007. http://www.cinemaspy.com/article.php?id=379.

Feffer, John. "The Undead and Us." *Foreign Policy in Focus*, November 13, 2013. http://fpif.org/undead-us/.

Ferguson, Charles, dir. *Inside Job*. New York: Sony Pictures Classics, 2010.

Fernández Gonzalo, Jorge. *Filosofía zombi*. Barcelona: Anagrama, 2011.

Ford, Martin. *Rise of the Robots: Technology and the Threat of a Jobless Future*. New York: Basic Books, 2015.

FP Staff. "The 2013 Failed States Index—Interactive Map and Rankings." *Foreign Policy (FP)*, June 24, 2013. http://foreignpolicy.com/2013/06/24/the-2013-failed-states-index-interactive-map-and-rankings/.

Freedman, Carl. *The Incomplete Projects: Marxism, Modernity, and the Politics of Culture*. Middletown, CT: Wesleyan University Press, 2002.

Gelder, Ken. "Introduction to Part 5." In *The Horror Reader*, edited by Ken Gelder. New York: Routledge, 2000.

Gillings, Joseph. "We're Obsessed with Zombies—Which Says a Lot About Today." *The Conversation*, February 23, 2015. https://theconversation.com/were-obsessed-with-zombies-which-says-a-lot-about-today-37552.

Giroux, Henry A. *Zombie Politics and Culture in the Age of Casino Capitalism*. New York: Peter Lang, 2011.

González, Házael. *La muerte negra: El triunfo de los no muertos*. Palma de Mallorca: Dolmen, 2010.

———. *Quijote Z*. Palma de Mallorca, Spain: Dolmen, 2010.

Grahame-Smith, Seth. *Abraham Lincoln Vampire Hunter*. New York: Grand Central Publishing, 2010.

———. *Pride and Prejudice and Zombies*. Philadelphia, PA: Quirk Productions, 2009.

Greer, Margaret. *Maria de Zayas Tells Baroque Tales of Love and the Cruelty of Men (Studies in Romance Literatures)*. University Park, PA: Pennsylvania State University Press, 2000.

Grimm, Fred. "Fear, Anxiety Drive Zombie Craze." *The Miami Herald*, June 5, 2012. http://www.miamiherald.com/news/special-reports/causeway-attack/article1940366.html.

Guma, Greg. "Schwarzenegger, DSK, and Gingrich: Do We Have Psychopaths Misruling Our World?" *Alternet*, May 19, 2011, http://www.alternet.org/story/151014/schwarzenegger,_dsk,_and_gingrich%3A_do_we_have_psychopaths_misruling_our_world.

Hagerstrand, Torsten. *Innovation Diffusion as a Spatial Process*. Chicago: University of Chicago Press, 1967.

Hand, Richard J. "Proliferating Horrors: Survival Horror and the *Resident Evil* Franchise." In *Horror Film: Creating and Marketing Fear*, edited by Steffen Hantke. Jackson, MS: University Press of Mississippi, 2009.

Haraway, Donna. "The Promises of Monsters: A Regenerative Politics for Inappropriate/d Others." In *Cultural Studies*, edited by Lawrence Grossberg, Cary Nelson, and Paula A. Treichler. New York: Routledge, 1992.

Hardin, Garrett. "The Tragedy of the Commons." *Science* 162, no. 3859 (December 13, 1968): 1243–8.

Hardt, Michael and Antonio Negri. *Multitude: War and Democracy in the Age of Empire*. New York: Penguin Books, 2004.

Hari, Johann. "It's Not Just Dominique Strauss-Kahn. The IMF Itself Should Be on Trial." *The Independent*, June 3, 2011. http://www.independent.co.uk/voices/commentators/johann-hari/johann-hari-its-not-just-dominique-strausskahn-the-imf-itself-should-be-on-trial-2292270.html.

Harman, Chris. *Zombie Capitalism: Global Crisis and the Relevance of Marx*. Chicago: Haymarket Books, 2010.

Harvey, David. *A Brief History of Neoliberalism*. New Yoro: Oxford University Press, 2005.

———. *The Enigma of Capital*. New York: Oxford University Press, 2010.

Hayles, Katherine. *How We Became Posthuman: Virtual Bodies in Cybernetics, Literature and Informatics*. Chicago: University of Chicago Press, 1999.

Heffernan, Kevin. "Inner-City Exhibition and the Genre Film: Distributing *Night of the Living Dead* (1968)." *Cinema Journal* 41, no. 3 (2002): 59–77.

Hirst, Paul, and Grahame Thompson. "The Future of Globalization." *Cooperation and Conflict: Journal of the Nordic International Studies Association* 37, no. 3 (2002): 247–65.

Hobbes, Thomas, and J. C. A. Gaskin. *Leviathan*. 1651. Oxford: Oxford University Press, 1998.

Homer-Dixon, Thomas. *The Ingenuity Gap*. New York: Knopf Publishing, 2000.

———. "Environmental Scarcities and Violent Conflict: Evidence from Cases." *International Security* 19, no. 1 (Summer 1994): 5–40.

"How Will You Communicate in a Zombie Attack?" *Everbridge*. Accessed September 2, 2015, http://www.everbridge.com/how-will-you-communicate-in-a-zombie-attack/?mkt_tok=3RkMMJWWfF9wsRogu67BZKXonjHpfsX56eklW7Hro8Yy0EZ5VunJEUWy20QJTNQ%2FcOedCQkZHblFnVwITq2kT6sNrKcJ.

Huet, Marie-Hélene. "Introduction to *Monstrous Imagination*." In *The Horror Reader*, edited by Ken Gelder. New York: Routledge, 2000.

I Am Legend. Directed by Francis Lawrence. Burbank, CA: Warner Bros. Pictures, 2007.

Independence Day. Directed by Roland Emmerich. Los Angeles: 20th Century Fox, 1996.

Invasion of the Body Snatchers. Directed by Don Siegel. Los Angeles: Allied Artists Pictures Corporation, 1956.

Kant, Immanuel. *Critique of the Power of Judgment*, edited by Paul Guyer and translated by Paul Guyer and Eric Matthews. Cambridge: Cambridge University Press, 2000.

Kaplan, Robert D. *The Coming Anarchy: Shattering the Dreams of the Post Cold War World*. New York: Vintage, 2000.

King, Stephen. *Cell: A Novel*. New York: Scribner Publishing, 2006.

Kirkman, Robert. *The Walking Dead*. Berkeley, CA: Image Comics, 2003–.

Kristeva, Julia. *Powers of Horror: An Essay on Abjection*, translated by León Roudiez. New York: Columbia University Press, 1982.

Lacan, Jacques. *Ecrits*, translated by Bruce Fink. New York: Norton, 2002.

Landis, Geoffrey. "Dead Right." In *The Ultimate Zombie*, edited by Byron Preiss and John Betancourt. New York: Dell, 1993.

Land of the Dead. Directed by George Romero. Universal City, CA: Universal Pictures, 2005.

The Last Man on Earth. Directed by Ubaldo Ragona and Sidney Salkow. Los Angeles: American International Pictures, 1964.

"The Last Man on Earth." *The Internet Movie Database (IMDb)*. Accessed December 1, 2008. http://www.imdb.com/title/tt0058700/.

Loureiro, Manel. *Apocalipsis Z*. Palma de Mallorca, Spain: Dolmen, 2007.

———. *Apocalypse Z: The Beginning of the End*, translated by Pamela Carmell. New York: AmazonCrossing, 2012.

Luhmann, Niklas. "Globalization or World Society? How to Conceive of Modern Society." *International Review of Sociology* 7, no. 1 (1997): 67.

Makuch, Eddie. "Resident Evil HD Breaks Sales Records." *GameSpot*, February 9, 2015. http://www.gamespot.com/articles/resident-evil-hd-breaks-sales-records/1100-6425190/.

Maravall, José Antonio. *La cultura del barroco: Análisis de una estructura histórica*. Barcelona: Ariel, 1975.

Martín, Manuel. *Noche de difuntos del 38*. Palma de Mallorca: Dolmen, 2012.

Marx, Karl. "Chapter Ten: The Working-Day." In *Capital, Volume One*. *Marxists Internet Archive*. Accessed June 2, 2015. https://www.marxists.org/archive/marx/works/1867-c1/ch10.htm.

Marx, Karl and Friedrich Engels. *The Communist Manifesto*. New York: Pocket Books, 1964.

Matheson, Richard. *I Am Legend*. New York: Fawcett Publications, 1954.

The Matrix. Directed by Larry Wachowski and Andy Wachowski. Burbank, CA: Warner Bros., 1999.

McConnell, Mariana. "Interview: George A. Romero on Diary of the Dead." *Cinema Blend*, January 14, 2008. http://www.cinemablend.com/new/Interview-George-A-Romero-On-Diary-Of-The-Dead-7818.html.

McKibben, Bill. "Global Warming's Terrifying New Math." *Rolling Stone Magazine*, July 19, 2012. http://www.rollingstone.com/politics/news/global-warmings-terrifying-new-math-20120719.

McRobert, Neil. "'Shoot Everything That Movies': Post-Millennial Zombie Cinema and the War on Terror." *Textus* 25, no. 3 (2012): 103–16.

Meadows, Donella H., Gary Meadows, Jorgen Randers, and William W. Behrens III. *The Limits to Growth*. New York: Universe Books, 1972.

Medrano, Julián de. *La silva curiosa*. edited by Mercedes Alcalá Galán. New York: Peter Lang, 1998.

Melton, J. Gordon. *The Vampire Book: The Encyclopedia of the Undead*. Canton, MI: Visible Ink Press, 1998.

Migoya, Hernán. *Una, grande y zombie*. Barcelona: Ediciones B, 2011.

Mizejewski, David. "Zombies vs. Animals? The Living Dead Wouldn't Stand a Chance." *Boing Boing*, October 14, 2013. http://boingboing.net/2013/10/14/zombiesvsanimals.html.

Monleón, José. *A Specter Is Haunting Europe: A Sociohistorical Approach to the Fantastic*. Princeton: Princeton University Press, 1990.

Moretti, Franco. "Dialectic of Fear (Extract)." In *The Horror Reader*, edited by Ken Gelder. New York: Routledge, 2000.

Morozov, Evgeny. "The Perils of Perfection." *New York Times*, March 2, 2013. http://www.nytimes.com/2013/03/03/opinion/sunday/the-perils-of-perfection.html?_r=1.

Morrill, Richard, Gary L. Gaile, and Grant Ian Thrall. *Spatial Diffusion*. Newbury Park, CA: Sage Publications, 1988.

Mortal Kombat. Directed by Paul W. S. Anderson. Los Angeles, CA: New Line Cinema, 1995.

Munz, Philip, et al. "When Zombies Attack!: Mathematical Modelling of an Outbreak of Zombie Infection." In *Infectious Disease Modelling Research Progress*, edited by Jean Michel Tchuenche and Christinah Chiyaka. New York: Nova Science Publishers, Inc., 2009.

Murphy, Bernice M. *The Suburban Gothic in American Popular Culture*. Hampshire, UK: Palgrave Macmillan, 2009.

Naim, Moises. "5 Wars of Globalization." *Foreign Policy*, January/February 2004, 28–37.

Newitz, Annalee. *Pretend We're Dead: Capitalist Monsters in American Pop Culture*. Durham, NC: Duke University Press, 2006.

Night of the Comet. Directed by Thom Eberhardt. Boston, MA/Los Angeles, CA: Atlantic Releasing Corporation, 1984.

Night of the Day of the Dawn of the Son of the Bride of the Return of the Revenge of the Terror of the Attack of the Evil, Mutant, Alien, Flesh Eating, Hellbound, Zombified Living Dead Part 2: In Shocking 2-D. Directed by Lowell Mason. New Jersey: Palmer Video (store chain), 1991.

Night of the Living Dead. Directed by George A. Romero. New York: The Walter Reade Organization, 1968.

Night of the Living Dead. Directed by Tom Savini. Los Angeles, CA: Columbia Pictures, 1990.

Nosferatu. Directed by F. W. Murnau. Berlin: Prana-Film GmbH, 1922.

Nosferatu. Directed by Werner Herzog. Munich: Werner Herzog Filmproduktion, 1979.

Office of Public Health Preparedness and Response. "Zombie Preparedness." *The Centers for Disease Control and Prevention*, last updated April 10, 2015, http://www.cdc.gov/phpr/zombies.htm.

The Omega Man. Directed by Boris Sagal. Burbank, CA: Warner Bros., 1971.

Paffenroth, Kim. *Gospel of the Living Dead: George Romero's Visions of Hell on Earth*. Waco, TX: Baylor University Press, 2006.

Peisner, David. "Blood, Sweat, & Zombies." *Rolling Stone*, October 24, 2013.

Pepperell, Robert. *The Posthuman Condition: Consciousness Beyond the Brain*. Portland, OR: Intellect Books, 2003.

Phillips, Erica E. "Zombie Studies Gain Ground on College Campuses: Students, Professors Study Culture of Living Dead." *Wall Street Journal*, March 3, 2014. http://online.wsj.com/news/articles/SB10001424052702304851104579361451951384512.

Picart, Caroline J. S. "The Third Shadow and Hybrid Genres: Horror, Humor, Gender and Race in Alien Resurrection." *Communication and Critical/Cultural Studies* 1, no. 4 (2004): 335–54.

Prokopy, Steve. "AICN Exclusive: Capone chews it with George Romero in first extended interview regarding Land of the Dead!" *Ain't It Cool News*, July 19, 2004. http://www.aintitcool.com/node/17989.

Re-Animator. Directed by Stuart Gordon. Los Angeles: Empire International Pictures, 1985.

Resident Evil. Directed by Paul W. S. Anderson. Culver City, CA: Columbia Pictures, 2002.

The Return of the Living Dead. Directed by Dan O'Bannon. Los Angeles, CA: Orion Pictures, 1985.

Return of the Living Dead Part II. Directed by Ken Wiederhorn. Culver City, CA: Lorimar Pictures, 1988.

Return of the Living Dead 3. Directed by Lawrence Steven Meyers, et al. Santa Monica, CA: Trimark Pictures, 1993.

Return of the Living Dead 4: Necropolis. Directed by Ellory Elkayem. Beverly Hills, CA, 2005.

Revolution. Created by Eric Kripke. Burbank, CA: Warner Bros. Television Distribution, 2012.

Rice, Anne. *Interview with the Vampire*. New York: Random House, 1976.

Rogers, Everett M. *Diffusion of Innovations*, 4th ed. New York: Free Press, 1985.

Romero, George A. "Preface to John Russo." In John Russo, *Night of the Living Dead*, New York: Warner Books, 1974.

Roth, Veronica. "Bonus Materials," In *Divergent*. New York: Katherine Tegen Books, 2011.

Shaun of the Dead. Directed by Edgar Wright. Universal City, CA: Universal Pictures, 2004.

Shaviro, Steven. *The Cinematic Body*. Minneapolis: University of Minnesota Press, 1993.

Sherwin, Richard K. *Visualizing Law in the Age of the Digital Baroque: Arabesques & Entanglements*. New York: Routledge, 2011.

Silent Hill. Directed by Christophe Gans. Culver City, CA: TriStar Pictures, 2006.

Silver, Alain, and James Ursini. *The Zombie Film: From White Zombie to World War Z*. Milwaukee, WI: Applause Theatre & Cinema, 2014.

Simmons, Beth A. and Zachary Elkins. "The Globalization of Liberalization: Policy Diffusion in the International Political Economy." *American Political Science Review* 98, no. 1 (2004): 171–89.

Sisí, Carlos. *Los Caminantes*. Palma de Mallorca, Spain: Dolmen, 2011.

Skipp, John. *Zombies: Encounters with the Hungry Dead*. New York: Black Dog and Leventhal Publishers, 2009.

Sloth, T. E. and David Wong. "5 Scientific Reasons a Zombie Apocalypse Could Actually Happen." *Cracked*. Accessed October 29, 2007, http://www.cracked.com/article_15643_5-scientific-reasons-zombie-apocalypse-could-actually-happen.html#ixzz2yInzMXq7.

Stoker, Bram. *Dracula: Authoritative Text, Backgrounds, Reviews and Reactions, Dramatic and Film Variations, Criticism*. Ed. Nina Auerbach and David J. Skal. New York: Norton & Company, 1997.

Survival of the Dead. Directed by George A. Romero. Toronto, Ontario: E1 Entertainment, 2009.

The Terminator. Directed by James Cameron. Los Angeles: Orion Pictures, 1984.

Thomson, Janice. *Mercenaries, Pirates, and Sovereigns: State-Building and Extraterritorial Violence in Early Modern Europe*. Princeton, NJ: Princeton University Press, 1994.

Tollefson, Ted E. "Cinemyths: Contemporary Films as Gender Myth." In *Soul of Popular Culture: Looking at Contemporary Heroes, Myths, and Monsters*, edited by Lynn Kittelson. Peru, IL: Open Court, 1998.

Torquemada, Antonio de. *Jardín de flores curiosas*, edited by Giovanni Allegra. Madrid: Castalia, 1982.

True Blood. Created by Alan Ball. New York: HBO, 2008.

Turner, Graham. "A Comparison of 'The Limits to Growth' with Thirty Years of Reality." *Commonwealth Scientific and Industrial Research Organisation (CSIRO)*. CSIRO Working Paper Series 2008–9, Working Paper No. 1834–5638 (June 2008).

Twilight. Directed by Catherine Hardwicke. Universal City, CA: Summit Entertainment, 2008.

The Vampire Diaries. Developed by Kevin Williamson and Julie Plec. Burbank, CA: Warner Bros. Television Distribution, 2009.

Van Creveld, Martin. *The Transformation of War*. New York: Free Press, 1991.

Vulliamy, ed. "The Drug War Is the Inevitable Result of Capitalism Gone Mad; Ciudad Juarez Is All of Our Futures." *Alternet*. Accessed June 21, 2011. http://www.alternet.org/story/151361/the_drug_war_is_the_inevitable_result_of_capitalism_gone_mad%3B_ciudad_juarez_is_all_of_our_futures.

Waldman, Paul. "The Left and the Living Dead: In the Event of a Zombie Apocalypse, Will Progressive Ideals Win Out?" *The American Prospect*. Accessed June 16, 2009. http://prospect.org/article/left-and-living-dead.

The Walking Dead. Developed by Frank Darabont. New York: AMC Studios, 2010.

Waller, Gregory A. *The Living and the Undead: From Stoker's Dracula to Romero's Dawn of the Dead*. Urbana, IL: University of Illinois Press, 1986.

Warm Bodies. Directed by Jonathan Levine. Universal City, CA: Summit Entertainment, 2013.

Wasik, Bill and Monica Murphy. *Rabid: A Cultural History of the World's Most Diabolical Virus*. New York: Penguin Books, 2012.

Watson, Julie. "'Zombie Apocalypse' Training Drill Organized By Halo Corp. For Military, Police Set for Oct. 31 in San Diego." *Associated Press*, October 27, 2012. http://www.huffingtonpost.com/2012/10/29/zombie-apocalypse-trainining-military-halo-corp-_n_2036996.html.

The Week Staff. "America's $5 Billion Zombie Industry: By the Numbers." *The Week*, October 27, 2011. http://theweek.com/article/index/220774/americas-5-billion-zombie-industry-by-the-numbers.

Wellington, David. *Monster Island, A Zombie Novel*. New York: Thunder's Mouth Press, 2006.

Williamsen, Amy. "Challenging the Code: Honor in María de Zayas." In *María de Zayas: The Dynamics of Discourse*, edited by Amy Williamsen and Judith Whitenack. Madison, NJ: Fairleigh Dickinson University Press, 1995.

Williams, Evan Calder. *Combined and Uneven Apocalypse*. Winchester, UK: Zero Books, 2011.

White Zombie. Directed by Victor Halperin. Beverly Hills, CA: United Artists, 1932.

Williams, Tony. *The Cinema of George Romero: Knight of the Living Dead*. London: Wallflower Press, 2003.

Wilmington, Mike, and Barry Brown. "Interview: George Romero, Knight of the Living Dead." *High Times* 71 (1981): 36.

"World War Z." *Box Office Mojo*. Accessed September 2, 2015. http://www.boxofficemojo.com/movies/?id=worldwarz.htm.

Wright, Gordon. *The Ordeal of Total War, 1939–1945*. Scranton, PA: Harper Collins, 1968.

Zayas, María de. *Desengaños amorosos*, edited by Alicia Yllera. Madrid: Cátedra, 1983.

Žižek, Slavoj. *Living in the End Times*. New York: Verso, 2011.

———. *Organs Without Bodies: On Deleuze and Consequences*. New York: Routledge, 2004.

———. *The Ticklish Subject: The Absent Centre of Political Ontology*. London: Verso, 1999.

———. *Violence: Six Sideways Reflections*. London: Profile Books, 2008.

"Zombie Apocalypse Survival Gear." *True Swords*. Accessed September 2, 2015, http://www.trueswords.com/zombie_apocalypse.php.

Zombie Survival Army-Navy Supplies. Accessed September 2, 2015, http://www.zombiesurvivalorlando.com/.

Zombieland. Directed by Ruben Fleischer. Los Angeles, CA: Columbia Pictures, 2009.

Zombies: The Truth. Directed by Mike Wafer. Washington, D.C.: National Geographic Channel, 2010.

Zombie Tools (ZT). Accessed September 2, 2015. http://www.zombietools.net/.

ZRS Staff, "Worst Country for Zombie Survival." *Zombie Research Society*, February 14, 2012, http://zombieresearchsociety.com/archives/2606.

Index

28 Days Later, 24, 25, 26, 74, 79, 80, 93, 98
28 Weeks Later, 24, 81, 85, 98
9/11, *see* September 11 (2001)

Adkins, Brent, 21
Adorno, Theodor, 3
African American Studies, 3, 97, 90n45
Ben (character), 20–1, 22, 67
AIDS, 69, 110
apocalypse, 2, 3, 4, 7, 26, 27, 48, 50, 53, 54, 59, 64, 65, 69, 73, 74, 75, 76, 82, 83, 84–5, 85–6, 89n30, 95, 106, 110–111, 112
post-apocalypse, 2, 4, 7, 51–3, 55, 64, 87, 109

Badiou, Alain, 98, 105–106
Bakan, Joel, 103, 104
Barber, Benjamin, 73, 74, 75
Barber, Paul, 10
Benedict, Barbara, 41
Berenstein, R. J., 12
Bird, Elizabeth, 49
Birds, The, 23, 35n13
Bishop, Kyle, 26, 49, 95, 109
Booker, M. Keith, 74
Boyle, Danny, 25, 26
Brooks, Max, *see World War Z* (2006)
Browning, John Edgar, viii, 1–8, 9–38, 46, 48, 53, 67, 73, 75, 93, 109

Brown, Lawrence, 77

capitalism, 3–4, 7, 16, 18, 20, 23, 46, 50, 61n26, 73, 75, 85, 95–6, 97, 98–9, 101, 104, 112, 113
anti-capitalism, 14, 17, 18
global capitalism, 3, 6, 23, 59, 111
Carr, Nicholas, 3
Carroll, Noël, 13, 17, 33
Castillo, David R., viii–ix, 1–8, 39–62, 73, 75, 110, 113
CDC (The Centers for Disease Control and Prevention), 48–9, 65
Cervantes, Miguel de, 56, 57, 58, 59
Cohen, Jeffrey Jerome, 95
Conde, Victor, 54–5
Creveld, Martin Van, 71

Dawn of the Dead (1978), 2, 6, 12, 14, 16, 21–2, 25, 34, 50, 90n45
Dawn of the Dead (2004), 22, 26
Day of the Dead, 16, 22, 25, 51, 80
Deleuze, Gilles, 20, 35n1
Dennett, Daniel C., 19
diffusion, 7, 76, 77–8, 82
Doc of the Dead, 25
Doomsday, 24, 26
Dracula, 18, 27, 35n3, 42, 43, 44, 45, 60n12, 105

Egginton, William, ix, 108–114
Engels, Friedrich, *see* Marxism
electronic gaming, *see* video game

Feffer, John, 66, 73
Freedman, Carl, 10, 12

Gelder, Ken, 44
Gillings, Joseph, 66
Giroux, Henry, 96
globalization, 6, 7, 59, 69–76, 77–8, 85, 86, 89n30, 103, 111
global neoliberalism, *see* neoliberalism
Gonzalo, Jorge Fernández, 59
Gothic, 11, 12, 23, 41, 42
Grahame-Smith, Seth, *see* Pride and Prejudice and Zombies
Gramsci, Antonio, 97–8
Guattari, Félix, 20, 35n1

Hagerstrand, Torsten, 77
Hand, Richard J. 23, 24, 35n12
Haraway, Donna, 94
Hardt, Michael, 94, 101
Hari, Johann, 101–102
Harman, Chris, 96, 105
Harvey, David, 99, 101, 105
Heffernan, Kevin, 17, 19
homosexuality, *see* sexuality
Horkheimer, Max, 3

I Am Legend (1954), 5–6, 10, 11, 12, 13, 15, 16, 18, 19, 27, 33–4, 35n3, 48, 67, 74, 80, 83, 84, 109, 112
print history of, 10, 27–33
I Am Legend (2007), 12, 80
Invasion of the Body Snatchers, 68, 78

Kaplan, Robert D., 69–70, 72, 73
Kant, Immanuel, 111, 112
Kirkman, Robert, 25, 26, 59

Land of the Dead, 2, 3, 22, 50, 51, 53
Last Man on Earth, The, 11, 19, 35n7
Lazarillo de Tormes, 56–7, 58
Loureiro, Manel, 53–4

Luhmann, Niklas, 111

Marxism, 3, 15, 43, 75, 95, 109, 113
Marx, Karl, *see* Marxism
Matheson, Richard, 4, 5, 6, 11, 12, 13, 14, 16, 19, 22, 23, 25, 33, 34, 35n6–7, 48
Matrix, The, 48, 113
media literacy, 2–4
Melton, Gordon, J., 35n6
Migoya, Hernán, 57, 58, 59
monstrosity, 4, 6, 7–8, 13, 17, 40–2, 43, 44, 45, 46, 47, 49, 53, 57, 59, 60n12, 73, 76, 78, 79, 93, 94, 96, 97, 99, 100, 103, 104–105, 109, 110, 112
see also teratology
Morozov, Evgeny, 3–4
Murphy, Bernice M., 12
Murphy, Monica, 69, 89n19

Naturaleza muerta, 5, 54–6
Negri, Antonio, 94, 101
Newitz, Annalee, 95, 96
Night of the Comet, 25
Night of the Living Dead (1968), 6, 12–13, 14, 15–21, 23, 25, 33, 48, 57, 66, 67, 68, 75, 78, 79, 83, 90n44, 97, 109
Night of the Living Dead (1990), 22
neoliberalism, 3, 7, 8, 93, 94, 96, 98, 98–99, 100, 101, 102, 104–105, 106, 109–110

Omega Man, The, 12

Paffenroth, Kim, 13–14
Picart, Caroline J. S., 12, 14
post-millennialism, 24–7, 34, 113
Pride and Prejudice and Zombies, 5, 50, 64
psychopath, 7, 99–100, 101, 102, 103, 104, 109–110
psychosexualism, 46

Re-Animator, 80, 89n19
Reilly, David A., ix, 7, 63–91, 110–111, 113
Resident Evil (films), franchise of, 22, 24, 79

Resident Evil (games), franchise of, 23–4, 64, 82
Riolan, Jean, 40
Robert Neville (character), 11–12, 13, 19, 25, 84, 90n45
Rogers, Everett, 77
Romero, George A., 2, 3, 4, 5, 6, 11, 13–14, 15, 16, 17, 18, 19, 22, 23, 24, 25, 33, 34, 36n22, 47, 48, 50, 51, 53, 54, 57, 67–8, 69, 80, 88n19, 89n30
Roth, Veronica, 52

Schmid, David, ix–x, 7–8, 49, 92–107, 109
Schlozman, Steven, 65
September 11 (2001), 25, 26, 49, 68, 95
sexuality, 40, 46, 69
  bisexuality, 93
  homosexuality, 57, 93
  lesbianism, 93
Shaviro, Steven, 15, 16, 36n22
Sherwin, Richard K., 2
shopping mall, 3, 16, 21, 22, 26, 34, 50
Silent Hill, 23–4
Sisi, Carlos, 53–4
survival
  communal action, 18, 19, 20, 21, 22, 34
survival horror (genre), *see* video game
survival space, 4, 5, 6, 13–26, 33–4, 112
and ambulation, 27, 34

teratology, 6, 11, 12, 13, 41
Tollefson, Ted E., 14

United Nations Security Council, 65
US Department of Homeland Security, 64, 65

vampire, 5, 6, 8, 10, 11, 19, 42–6, 48–9, 56, 57, 60n12, 67, 69, 88n19, 90n45, 96, 98, 104
revenant, 10
video game, 6, 8, 11, 14, 22–4, 26, 33, 48, 59, 64, 82
visual literacy, *see* media literacy

Waldman, Paul, 93
Walking Dead, The, 5, 25, 26, 27, 48, 51, 52, 53, 59
Waller, Gregory A., 13, 15, 16, 18–19, 20, 33–4
War on Drugs, 72
War on Terror, 49, 72
Wasik, Bill, 69, 88
White Zombie, 5, 10, 46, 47, 78, 89n30
Williams, Even Calder, 97, 98, 101
Williams, Tony, 14
World War Z (2006), 48, 74, 79–80, 83, 84, 90n47
World War Z (2011), 64, 80

Zayas, María de, 5, 47–8
Žižek, Slavoj, 3, 15, 34, 61n26, 98–9
zombie(s)
  African and Haitian, 46, 48
  and class, 3
  domesticization of, 10, 12
  massing of, 2–3, 4, 5, 6, 13, 14, 15, 19, 21, 33, 35n12, 46, 48, 49, 50, 51, 53, 59, 76–8, 85
  phenomenon (or renaissance or craze), 4, 5, 6, 8, 34, 48–9, 58, 59, 61n25, 73, 76, 83, 109
  topos of, 2, 7, 23
Zombie Research Society, 83
Zombie Survival Guide, The, 26, 64

CPSIA information can be obtained
at www.ICGtesting.com
Printed in the USA
LVHW091838231118
597791LV00007BA/166/P